Prairie State Books

In conjunction with the Illinois Center for the Book, the University of Illinois Press is reissuing in paperback works of fiction and nonfiction that are, by virtue of authorship and/or subject matter, of particular interest to the general reader in the state of Illinois.

A list of books in the series appears at the end of this volume.

Mr. Dooley in Peace and in War

MR. DOOLEY IN PEACE AND IN WAR

Finley Peter Dunne

Introduction by Paul Green

UNIVERSITY OF ILLINOIS PRESS
Urbana and Chicago

Introduction © 1988 by the Board of Trustees of the University of Illinois
Manufactured in the United States of America
P 5 4 3 2 1

This book is printed on acid-free paper.

Library of Congress Cataloging-in-Publication Data

Dunne, Finley Peter, 1867-1936.
  Mr. Dooley in peace and in war.

  (Prairie State books)
  Bibliography: p.
  I. Title. II. Series.
PN6161.D82 1988   814'.52   88-20662
ISBN 0-252-06040-7 (alk. paper)

Contents

MR. DOOLEY IN PEACE

Introduction

MR. MARTIN J. DOOLEY is the philosopher laureate of Chicago. Created by Chicago newspaperman Finley Peter Dunne in the 1890s, Mr. Dooley reflected the coming of age of Chicago ethnics. As the fictional saloonkeeper of an "Archey Road" (Archer Avenue) drinking establishment on the city's near southwest side, Dooley commented on the passing local and national scene with the precision of a baseball umpire: "he called them as the saw them."

In over 300 columns Mr. Dooley's wit and wisdom enlightened and entertained a vast reading audience. *Mr. Dooley: In Peace and in War* (originally published in 1898) was the first collection of Dooley columns published in book form. An instant best-seller, this book provided Dunne not only national recognition but a career move to New York City. He would never work again in Chicago.

Who Was Finley Peter Dunne?

Dunne was born in 1867 on the near west side of Chicago. His father, Peter, was an Irish immigrant from Queens County (today known as Laois County), Ireland, whose trade as a carpenter gave the family a middle-class lifestyle. His mother, Ellen Finley Dunne, was "widely read in English fiction"[1] and created a bookish atmosphere in the Dunne household. It is interesting to note that from his early childhood to his old age, Dunne lived a life far different from the working-class people he wrote about in his original Mr. Dooley columns. Moreover, as the Irish would say, Dunne was actually a "sneaking regarder" of mainline, Protestant society. After leaving Chicago he strove to be friends of New York City's rich and powerful—and though not wealthy he had a lifestyle as close to that of an urban gentleman as possible.

Though he never lost his Irishness and remained involved in various Irish causes, Dunne, throughout his professional life, would be more interested in writing about his people than living with them. In fact, throughout his entire life, he made only one visit to see his ancestral and literary roots in Ireland.

Dunne, an inferior high school student, jumped into a journalism career due in part to limited options. In 1884 he took his first newspaper job as an office boy and reporter for the *Chicago Telegram* (over the next decade and a half Dunne would work for five other Chicago daily newspapers). Quick on his feet and fast with a quip, Dunne became part of the vibrant and cutthroat Chicago journalism scene. As historian Barbara Schaaf has written, Chicago newspapers in the last part of the nineteenth century "fought for philosophical, political and geographic allegiance from their readers."[2] Dunne, ever ambitious, would establish a reputation as a political satirist in this highly charged atmosphere equal to that of fellow Chicago journalists such as George Ade, Theodore Dreiser, and Eugene Field.

In 1889 Dunne used a dialect style of reporting for the first time. His constant shifting between Chicago's newspapers resulted in his gaining more freedom to create his own column and characters. Following the appearance of his first Mr. Dooley column in 1893, Dunne's reputation increased in both Chicago and the nation. In the next seven years Dunne would produce his richest Dooley columns. His turn-of-the-century move to New York City gave him a wider audience and greater fame, but it also took away the heart of his Mr. Dooley columns—the Irish-neighborhood connection. According to his biographer Elmer Ellis, by shifting his vision to the national arena "no longer could Dunne utilize purely or primarily Chicago affairs for his comments, nor could he exploit local characters."[3]

Dunne would live in New York until his death in 1936. He would produce several more books, many more columns, and feature articles. He would mingle with presidents and financiers as he lived the good life—in between bouts of illness. Yet through it all his fame would rest on his periodic resurrection of his favorite fictional character, Mr. Dooley. Like a literary Edgar Bergen, Dunne used a prop to express his innermost thoughts and ideas. Bergen's Charlie McCarthy was Dunne's Mr. Dooley: the human creator of the unreal character was never as witty or clever on his own as he was through the actions or words of his fictional friend. Dunne's ventriloquism in prose was his vehicle for success.

Debate today continues over the accomplishments and contributions of Finley Peter Dunne. His sharpest critic, Charles Fanning, believes that Dunne wrote as a historian, literary realist, and philosopher. Moreover, it's Fanning's view that Dunne's style ranged from the American notions of cracker-barrel philosopher and tall-tale teller to the literary and folk traditions of Ireland.[4] Whatever the final analysis, Dunne gave the world Mr. Dooley, and through this legendary saloonkeeper we can see Irish Chicago in all its glory and pain.

Who Was Martin J. Dooley?

One Dunne commentator has called Mr. Dooley the "quintessential urbanite." Perhaps, but one must never underestimate the Irishness and the ethnic connection of America's favorite fictional saloonkeeper. The Dooley columns reveal the love-hate relationship between newcomers from different lands who could work together at low-level–low-income jobs but once in the security of their home neighborhoods attack each other verbally and physically for perceived ethnic favoritism, unique cultural habits, and general sport.

Mr. Dooley was the third fictional Irish character Dunne had trotted out before the public. Following in the footsteps of the less successful Colonel Thomas Jefferson Dolan and Colonel Malachi McNeery, Martin J. Dooley became an overnight celebrity.

Dooley's saloon was the "gin mill of residence" for Irish working men. Many of them were steady customers like John McKenna and Mr. Hennessey, who dropped by to share a few moments with their favorite saloonkeeper. Standing behind his bar, Martin J. Dooley, a sixtyish, confirmed bachelor and former precinct captain, commented on the local and national scene. Calling himself a saloonkeeper and Doctor of Philosophy, Mr. Dooley's world extended far beyond the neighborhood landmarks of Healey's slough and the local police station. Yet it was the community of Bridgeport and its people that impelled the Dooley character to greatness.

Dunne wrote his Dooley columns in a strange form of Irish dialect. The uniqueness of his presentation created as much interest as the content of Mr. Dooley's beliefs. Late in his life, Dunne explained that he started using mainly the dialect form of writing in 1892 to avoid the possibilities of lawsuits, because during this time Dunne was an editorial writer attacking city corruption for the *Chicago Post.* "It occurred to me," said Dunne, "that while it might be dangerous to call an alderman a thief in English no one could sue if a comic Irishman denounced the statesman as a thief . . . if I had written the same thing in English I would inevitably been pistoled or slugged."[5]

Whatever the purpose for using the dialect form of writing, Dooleyisms are almost as famous for how they are said as for their content. Though Irish-Irish (as opposed to American-Irish) then and now claim Dunne did not capture their country's speech patterns and that Dooley books were never popular in their country, it's hard to argue with the success and impact of his dialectal style. When Mr. Dooley uttered his first political commentary to John McKenna—that their evening's activities were "duller than a ray-publican primary in th' fouth ward"—dialect and Dooley became inseparable.

Why did Mr. Dooley become so popular? And why were so many people interested in a community like Bridgeport, which had started in the late 1830s as a squatters' village of Irish laborers and by the turn of the century had as its greatest feature Bubbly Creek (a name given to a small fork of the Chicago River that in the summer months unleashed an odor felt throughout the neighborhood)? The answer rests with the social, political, and economic role the Irish immigrants played, and were playing, in an ever-expanding ethnic Chicago.

Over three million Irish came to the United States in the years between the onset of the potato famine in the mid-1840s and the death of Charles Parnell in 1891.[6] The advanced guard entered Chicago prior to 1840 to work as laborers on the Illinois-Michigan canal and later the railroads. Groups of Irish settlers set up numerous so-called "shanty villages"—like Bridgeport—along the branches of the Chicago River.

Soon these low-income communities became high crime areas, and "hoodlum Irish" and "shanty Irish" became popular terms for Irish arrested for a variety of disorderly conduct crimes. The *Chicago Tribune,* a leading anti-Irish newspaper, as late as 1874 asked the following question, "Why are the instigators and ring leaders of our riots and tumults in nine cases out of ten, Irishmen?"[7]

It's important to note that not all Irish immigrants settled in American cities—it just seemed that way to other urban residents. By 1860 one-fourth of all American big-city dwellers were Irish; the sons and daughters of Erin would dominate the street life of urban America for the rest of the century.

On the surface the urbanization of the American Irish seemed odd since most Irish newcomers had emigrated from rural villages. Yet for those who understood Irish history this urban-oriented Irish-American settlement pattern was both logical and practical. The whole issue boiled down to one basic fact: the differences between rural living in the United States and Ireland were greater than the differences between living in urban America and rural Ireland. Incoming Irish believed the rural lifestyle in the United States was Protestant-dominated whereas in Ireland it was a Catholic tradition. This was no small belief on the part of the Irish newcomers, who saw their ethnicity defined mostly by their religion. Dunne himself would capture this belief when he was once asked if he were a Roman Catholic; his response was, "No, I'm a Chicago Catholic."[8]

Most Irish emigrating to America were poor. For troubled Ireland the departure of many of its economically disadvantaged citizens acted as a safety valve for those who remained, especially the middle class. Irish nationalists fighting British rule called the emigration forced exile (though only less than 10 percent would return to Ireland). A majority of the Irish immigrants to America came from western Ireland. They were more traditional in their Irish customs than were their more anglicized and modern compatriots living in the eastern part of the island. Thus, it was no coincidence that Dunne listed Roscommon as Mr. Dooley's home county in the old country. This rural, western area of Ireland was a fertile source for Irish immigrants coming to America.

The Irish immigrants' climb up the economic mobility ladder in Chicago was slow. They did not move quickly into professions or the skilled trades, and as late as 1870 a majority of the Irish workforce were unskilled laborers or domestics. Avenues opened to them were limited, but due to their numbers and time of arrival, public office and public employment became accessible and obtainable. In 1853 one-fourth of Chicago's elected officers were Irish; by 1865 the Irish made up one-third of the Chicgo Police department; and by 1890 a huge number of politically related jobs in law enforcement, fire service, sanitation, and transportation were held by Irish. No one handed the Irish this public path to better jobs, nor was it a conscious decision of incoming Irish immigrants, or their children, to find economic security in governmental service (a tradition severely limited by the British in Ireland). Rather, it was a road that seemed open, and given their restricted alternatives, the Irish took it.

As was seen in many Dooley columns, not all Irish Chicagoans were public employees. In fact, most of Dooley's patrons and neighbors worked the mills (various steel plants in the Chicago area), the yards (Union Stockyards), or the factories. The rungs of the mobility ladder seemed far apart for Chicago's Irish, and despite a slow process upward many were struggling, working-class poor at the end of the nineteenth century. However, to native Chicagoans and other nationalities, the Irish seemed to dominate government and thrive in politics. It was this economic "Paddy's paradox" that would filter through many Dunne columns. Mr. Dooley's customers' overall financial status did not reflect a level of monetary accomplishment or social acceptability that Irish critics believed they had achieved through their political influence and ethnic solidarity.

As the first poor mass migrants in Chicago, the Irish had been for years the city's dominant slum dwellers. Following the 1871 Great Fire, a flood of new immigrants from eastern and southern Europe joined the Irish (some of whom were at least second generation) in the city's poor neighborhoods. Knowing the ropes and being somewhat assimilated, the Irish became societal buffers between the strange-speaking newcomers and the native older citizens. In churches, factories, governmental bureaucracies, and political organizations the Irish achieved new status by communicating the process of assimilation to new arrivals.

Older ethnic groups, many of whom had assimilated far more easily into mainstream Chicago than the Irish, bristled at growing Irish influence in the city. The Illinois *Staats-Zeitung* lamented the fact that the Germans, though more numerous than the Irish, held far fewer elected offices: "German-Americans . . . are indifferent towards public affairs, but they may offer as an excuse for their lack of activity . . . the wild doings of the political Irish gang."[9] *Svenska-Tribunen Nyheter,* a Swedish daily, preceded future reform movements in Chicago against machine politics (which would often be a term synonymous with the Irish) by suggesting that "An Irish politician who can barely sign his own name, has a very decisive preference over a Swede, no matter how well educated and trained by experience a Swede might be."[10] It was in this ethnic, citywide climate that Martin J. Dooley and his philosophy would debut in the 1890s.

Through Dooley, Dunne's columns played with major aspects of Irish life in Bridgeport. Ever practical, and on the surface very cynical, Mr. Dooley would demonstrate an inner softness for the frustrations and failures of the Irish and an inner pride for their joys and accomplishments. Bridgeport was the key. "We are at once in that community," said Fanning on the Bridgeport-Dooley connection, "exposed to the flavor of a particular culture, where people are placed by family, geography, and reputation and where that placement carries real weight."[11] Bridgeport was a mind-frame to Dunne, and its ongoing evolution (eastern European newcomers moving into the community) and the very idea of technological progress itself reflected a sadness about the decline of a specific and special Irish place in Chicago.

On local urban politics Dunne's Dooley took a critical view of reformers that would also appear in future writings of Irishmen like James T. Farrell, Edwin O'Connor, Andrew Greeley, and Eugene Kennedy. Dooley was a pragmatist. He disliked the double-standard that allowed downtown business executives to rail publicly against corruption while they privately perpetuated it as a more profitable way to get things accomplished. Like many future Irish writers, Dunne also had disdain for government-reform zealots, many of whom were Protestant, who tried to change the structure and processes of city government because they disapproved of the type of people who were assuming political power. "Rayform the Rayformers" was a Dooley battle cry when he announced his own short-lived 1897 mayoral campaign. This motto also reflected the mood of the Bridgeporters, who saw public employment as being a cop on the beat or a person working the car (driving a street car), and they saw nothing wrong in using political clout to achieve their limited goals.

Dunne's social and political attitudes were those of Bridgeporters who, at best, were marginal people in Chicago "living on the fringe of society." Few could achieve the respectability and station of a downtown financier or lawyer. Thus, seldom does Mr. Dooley attack political corruption; instead, he is bemused by it. His real anger comes down on those who look down on his people and on those of his people who try to forget their roots by becoming "lace curtain" (uppity) Irish.

In this his first volume, Dunne reverses the *in Peace and in War* title in the book's content. The first third of the book allegedly deals with war, more specifically the conflict between the United States and Spain. This highlighting of national and international columns reflects Dunne's growing interest in American foreign policy. In his last few years as a Chicago columnist, Dunne concentrated heavily in this area as he attempted to expand his Bridgeport base. Through these columns Dunne translated international questions into "Dooleyisms" and simplified complicated issues by reducing them to Bridgeport terminology.

Dooley tried to cool down wartime emotionalism by revealing how the nation's leaders had actually mismanaged the Spanish-American crisis. He poked fun at some of the battles and politicians' attempts to capitalize on the war fever. In "On War Preparations," Dooley mocks the notion of this confrontation as a "splendid little war." He consistently denounces the imperialistic rhetoric that coincided with the war effort in many parts of the county. In critic Charles Fanning's views, Dunne was rebelling against America's grabbing of land from other people the way the British took away soil from the Irish. In perhaps his most outrageous effort to minimalize America's military overmatch against Spain, Dunne has Dooley call Admiral George Dewey (who along with Teddy Roosevelt was a great hero of the war) his cousin George. "Dewey or Dooley 'tis all the same," says the southside Chicago saloonkeeper. It was a commentary that brought both gasps and guffaws from Dunne's ever-expanding national readership.

Though national critics at the time praised the war part of this volume, it is the peace part, and specifically those pieces concentrating on Bridgeport and the Irish, that in the long run make this book a classic. Two particularly stand out. "On Criminals" is the hard-luck story of a young Irish lad named Petey Scanlan and his Irish mother. It is perhaps the most heartwrenching column Dooley ever wrote, and upon reading it today one can see the evolutionary beginnings of Studs Lonigan. It also conjures images of Jimmy Cagney, Pat O'Brien, and the Dead End Kids playing out an Irish melodrama in *Angels with Dirty Faces* or Cagney and O'Brien squaring off in the gangster movie *White Heat,* when hoodlum Cagney's only true friend was his Irish mother.

Young Scanlan's troubles are classic. Constantly in trouble with the law, Petey robs a grocery store, kills the owner, and escapes to his home while closely hounded by the police. A standoff ensues, but before any more violence takes place out steps Scanlan's mother, who confronts the authorities by asking, "Gintlemen what is it ye want in me. Liftinant Cassidy 'tis strange f'r ye that I've knowed so long to make scandal in me before me neighbors." Told of the day's events, Mrs. Scanlan brings out Petey, who refuses to let police touch him as he walks to the paddywagon on the arm of his mother. This sad story ends with Mrs. Scanlan sitting in the family's big chair with her apron in her hands and the picture of the lad in her lap.

"On Criminals" reflects the ever-present Irish desire for respectability, the challenges of growing up in a hard-nosed community like Bridgeport, and the risks of raising children in the big city—even if both parents are hard-working and God-fearing people. As Dooley says, "Who'll tell what makes wan man a thief or another man a saint." Life's unpredictability and sadness is played out alongside the nobility of Mrs. Scanlan's love for her son and her inner religious strength. This column also reflected Dunne's concerns about the price Irish-Americans were paying for assimilation. He saw an erosion of traditional Old World morality as the New World search for financial gain pushed some young Irish into a life of crime and violence.

Another masterpiece in this volume is "On the Power of Love." On the surface it's a commentary on the 1897 St. Patrick's Day championship fight between two Irish boxers, Bob Fitzsimmons and Jim Corbett, that ended when Fitzsimmons knocked out Corbett with his famous "solar plexus punch." However, on closer examination, this piece reveals Dunne as the ultimate realist, as he portrays Dooley as one of the few honest, even-tempered, and practical commentators of American life. It depicts one of Dunne's best efforts to attack hypocrisy, even if the latter emanates from the "fair sect" (women) or the church.

Mrs. Fitzsimmons's less-than-pure efforts to encourage her husband to win the match and Father Kelly's interest in the outcome of the "outhrajous affray" give Dunne the opportunity to attack conventional thinking and pomposity. He took special joy in revealing the phony self-righteousness of individuals who publicly condemn while they privately enjoy the pleasures of life. In this column he revealed that women could be as economically aggressive and physically threatening as any man (including the heavyweight champion of the world), and that the clergy were human beings who could not always practice what they preached.

Mr. Dooley in Peace and in War was social commentary written for the time. Its literary merits, dialect writing style aside, rest in Dunne's ability to express Irish working-class concerns (blue collar in today's vernacular) on vital local and national topics. It unlocked a source of sociopolitical insight from people whose views were seldom asked, let alone heard. In this book you can feel and see turn-of-the-century Chicago, smell the yards and street aromas, and, yes, if you try very hard, almost taste the foam of one of Mr. Dooley's special pints of suds. It also captures a special time in ethnic history when the Irish, filled with ambition for the future and covered with scars from the past, were ready to assume leadership of America's major cities. Carter H. Harrison II, Chicago's mayor at the time this book was published, captured the moment best when he said, "Among the Irish every grownup was a leader, a potential leader or anxious to lead."[12] In his own unique way Mr. Dooley was one of the first who announced to all, "Here come the Irish."

NOTES

1. Elmer Ellis, *Mr. Dooley's America: A Life of Finley Peter Dunne* (New York: Alfred A. Knopf, 1971), 6.

2. Barbara Schaaf, *Mr. Dooley's Chicago* (Garden City: Anchor/Doubleday, 1977), 5.

3. Ellis, 139.

4. Charles Fanning, *Finley Peter Dunne and Mr. Dooley: The Chicago Years* (Lexington: University Press of Kentucky, 1978), 219-20.

5. Dunne, Philip, ed., *Mr. Dooley Remembers—the Informal Memoirs of Finley Peter Dunne* (Boston: Little, Brown & Co., 1963), 270.

6. Thomas N. Brown, *Irish American Nationalism* (Philadelphia: Lippincott, 1966), 17.

7. *Chicago Tribune*, April 19, 1874.

8. Schaaf, 2.

9. Illinois *Staats-Zeitung*, April 21, 1892.

10. *Svenska Tribunen Nyheter*, October 6, 1906.

11. Fanning, 36.

12. Carter H. Harrison, *Growing Up with Chicago* (Chicago: R. F. Seymour, 1944), 24.

SUGGESTED READING

1. Dunne, Philip, ed. *Mr. Dooley Remembers—the Informal Memoirs of Finley Peter Dunne.* Boston: Little, Brown & Co., 1963.

2. Ellis, Elmer. *Mr. Dooley's America: A Life of Finley Peter Dunne.* New York: Alfred A. Knopf, 1971.

3. Fanning, Charles. *Finley Peter Dunne and Mr. Dooley: The Chicago Years.* Lexington: University Press of Kentucky, 1978.

4. McCaffrey, Lawrence J., Ellen Skerret, Michael Funchion, and Charles Fanning. *The Irish in Chicago.* Urbana: University of Illinois Press, 1987.

5. Schaaf, Barbara. *Mr. Dooley's Chicago.* Garden City: Anchor/Doubleday, 1977.

Preface

ARCHEY ROAD stretches back for many miles from the heart of an ugly city to the cabbage gardens that gave the maker of the seal his opportunity to call the city "urbs in horto." Somewhere between the two—that is to say, forninst th' gas-house and be-yant Healey's slough and not far from the polis station—lives Martin Dooley, doctor of philosophy.

There was a time when Archey Road was purely Irish. But the Huns, turned back from the Adriatic and the stock-yards and overrunning Archey Road, have nearly exhausted the orig-inal population,—not driven them out as they drove out less vigorous races, with thick clubs and short spears, but edged them out with the more biting weapons of modern civilization,—overworked and under-eaten them into more languid surround-ings remote from the tanks of the gashouse and the blast furnaces of the rolling-mill.

But Mr. Dooley remains, and enough remain with him to save the Archey Road. In this community you can hear all the various accents of Ireland, from the awkward brogue of the "far-downer" to the mild and aisy Elizabethan English of the southern Irish-man, and all the exquisite variations to be heard between Ar-magh and Bantry Bay, with the difference that would naturally arise from substituting cinders and sulphuretted hydrogen for soft misty air and peat smoke. Here also you can see the wakes and christenings, the marriages and funerals, and the other fêtes of the ol' counthry somewhat modified and darkened by American usage. The Banshee has been heard many times in Archey Road. On the eve of All Saints' Day it is well known that here alone the pookies play thricks in cabbage gardens. In 1893 it was reported that Malachi Dempsey was called "by the other people," and disappeared west of the tracks, and never came back.

A simple people! "Simple, says ye!" remarked Mr. Dooley. "Simple like th' air or th' deep sea. Not complicated like a watch that stops whin th' shoot iv clothes ye got it with wears out. Whin Father Butler wr-rote a book he niver finished, he said simplicity was not wearin' all ye had on ye'er shirt-front, like a tin-horn gambler with his di'mon' stud. An' 'tis so."

The barbarians around them are moderately but firmly governed, encouraged to passionate votings for the ruling race, but restrained from the immoral pursuit of office.

The most generous, thoughtful, honest, and chaste people in the world are these friends of Mr. Dooley, — knowing and innocent; moral, but giving no heed at all to patented political moralities.

Among them lives and prospers the traveller, archaeologist, historian, social observer, saloon-keeper, economist, and philosopher, who has not been out of the ward for twenty-five years "but twict." He reads the newspapers with solemn care, heartily hates them, and accepts all they print for the sake of drowning Hennessy's rising protests against his logic. From the cool heights of life in the Archey Road, uninterrupted by the jarring noises of crickets and cows, he observes the passing show, and mediates thereon. His impressions are transferred to the desensitized plate of Mr. Hennessy's mind, where they can do no harm.

"There's no betther place to see what's goin' on thin the Archey Road," says Mr. Dooley. "Whin th' ilicthric cars is hummin' down th' sthreet an' th' blast goin' sthrong at th' mills, th' noise is that gr-reat ye can't think."

He is opulent in good advice, as becomes a man of his station; for he has mastered most of the obstacles in a business career, and by leading a prudent and temperate life has established himself so well that he owns his own house and furniture, and is only slightly behind on his license. It would be indelicate to give statistics as to his age. Mr. Hennessy says he was a "grown man whin th' pikes was out in forty-eight, an' I was hedge-high, an' I'm near fifty-five." Mr. Dooley says Mr. Hennessy is eighty. He closes discussion on his own age with the remark, "I'm old enough to know betther." He has served his country with distinction. His conduct of the important office of captain of his precinct (1873-75) was highly commended, and there was some talk of nominating him for elderman. At the expiration of his term he was personally thanked by the Hon. M. McGee, at one time a member of the central committee. But the activity of public life was unsuited to a man of Mr. Dooley's tastes; and, while he continued to view the political situation always with interest and sometimes with alarm, he has resolutely declined to leave the bar for the forum. His early experience gave him wisdom in discussing public affairs. "Politics," he says, "ain't bean bag. 'Tis a man's game; an' women, childher, an' pro-hybitionists'd do well to keep out iv it." Again he remarks, "As Shakespeare says, 'Ol' men f'r th' council, young men f'r th' ward.' "

An attempt has been made in this book to give permanent form to a few of the more characteristic and important of Mr. Dooley's utterances. For permission to reprint the articles the thanks of the editor are due to Mr. George G. Booth, of the Chicago *Journal*, and to Mr. Dooley's constant friend, Mr. H. H. Kohlsaat, of the Chicago *Evening Post*.

F. P. D.

Mr. Dooley in War

On Diplomacy

"I'LL explain it to ye," said Mr. Dooley. " 'Tis this way. Ye see, this here Sagasta is a boonco steerer like Canada Bill, an' th' likes iv him. A smart man is this Sagasta, an' wan that can put a crimp in th' ca-ards that ye cudden't take out with a washer-woman's wringer. He's been through manny a ha-ard game. Talk about th' County Dimocracy picnic, where a three-ca-ard man goes in debt ivry time he hurls th' broads, 'tis nawthin' to what this here Spanish onion has been again an' beat. F'r years an' years he's played on'y profissionals. Th' la-ads he's tackled have more marked ca-ards in their pockets thin a preacher fr'm Mitchigan an' more bad money thin ye cud shake out iv th' coat-tail pockets iv a prosp'rous banker fr'm Injianny. He's been up again Gladstun an' Bisma-arck an' ol' what-ye-call-'im, th' Eye-talian, — his name's got away from me, — an' he's done thim all.

"Well, business is bad. No wan will play with him. No money's comin' in. Th' circus has moved on to th' nex' town, an' left him without a customer. Th' Jew man that loaned him th' bank-roll threatens to seize th' ca-ards on' th' table. Whin, lo an' behold, down th' sthreet comes a ma-an fr'm th' counthry, — a lawyer fr'm Ohio, with a gripsack in his hand. Oh, but he's a proud man. He's been in town long enough f'r to get out iv th' way iv th' throlley ca-ar whin th' bell rings. He's larned not to thry an' light his see-gaar at th' ilicthric light. He doesn't offer to pay th' ilivator ma-an f'r carryin' him upstairs. He's got so

3

he can pass a tall buildin' without thryin' f'r to turn a back summersault. An' he's as haughty about it as a new man on an ice-wagon. They'se nawthin' ye can tell him. He thinks iv himsilf goin' back to Canton with a r-red necktie on, an' settin' on a cracker box an' tellin' th' lads whin they come in fr'm pitchin' hor-rseshoes what a hot time he's had, an' how he's seen th' hootchy-kootchy an' th' Pammer House barber shop, an' th' other ondacint sight iv a gr-reat city.

"An' so he comes up to where Sagasta is kind iv throwin' th' ca-ards idly on th' top iv th' bar'l, an' Sagasta pipes him out iv th' corner iv his eye, an' says to himsilf: 'Oh, I dinnaw,' an' thanks hiven f'r th' law that has a sucker bor-rn ivry minyit. An' th' la-ad fr'm Canton thinks he can pick out th' Jack, an' sometimes he can an' sometimes he can't; but th' end iv it is th' Spanyard has him thrimmed down to his chest protector, an' he'll be goin' back to Canton in a blanket. Ye see it ain't his game. If it was pitchin' hor-rseshoes, 'twud be diff'rent. He cud bate Sagasta at that. He cud do him at rasslin' or chasin' th' greased pig, or in a wan-legged race or th' tug-iv-war. He cud make him look foolish at liftin' a kag iv beer or hitchin' up a team. But, whin it comes to di-plomacy, th' Spanyard has him again th' rail, an' counts on him till his ar-rm is sore."

"Why don't he tur-rn in an' fight?" demanded the patriotic Mr. Hennessy.

"Lord knows," said Mr. Dooley. "Mebbe 'twill tur-rn out th' way it did with two frinds iv mine. They was Joe Larkin an' a little r-red-headed man be th' name iv O'Brien, an' they wint out to th' picanic at Ogden's grove, where wanst a year Ireland's freed. They was a shell ma-an wurrukin' near th' fence, an' Larkin says, says he: 'He's aisy. Lave me have some money, an' we'll do him. I can see th' pea go undher th' shell ivry time.' So O'Brien bein' a hot spoort loaned him th' money, an' he wint at it. Ivry time Larkin cud see th' pea go undher th' shell as plain as day. Wanst or twict th' shell man was so careless that he left th' pea undher th' edge iv th' shell. But in five minyits all iv O'Brien's money was in th' bad ma-an's pockits, an' he was lookin' around f'r more foolish pathrites. It took O'Brien some time f'r to decide what to do. Thin says ye, 'Twas my money this fool blowed in.' An' he made a dash f'r th' shell ma'an; an' he not on'y got what he'd lost, but all th' r-rest iv th' capital besides. Ye see, that was his game. That was where he come in. An' he took th' money an' carrid it over to a corner iv th' gr-rounds where a la-ad had wan iv thim matcheens where ye pay tin cints f'r th' privilege iv seein' how har-rd ye can hit with a sledge-hammer, an' there he stayed till th' polis come arround to dhrive people off th' gr-rounds."

On War Preparations

"WELL," Mr. Hennessy asked, "how goes th' war?"

"Splendid, thank ye," said Mr. Dooley. "Fine, fine. It makes me hear-rt throb with pride that I'm a citizen iv th' Sixth Wa-ard."

"Has th' ar-rmy started f'r Cuba yet?"

"Wan ar-rmy, says ye? Twinty! Las' Choosdah an advance ar-rmy iv wan hundherd an' twinty thousand men landed fr'm th' Gussie, with tin thousand cannons hurlin' projick-tyles weighin' eight hundherd pounds sivinteen miles. Winsdah night a second ar-rmy iv injineers, miners, plumbers, an' lawn tinnis experts, numberin' in all four hundherd an' eighty thousand men, ar-rmed with death-dealin' canned goods, was hurried to Havana to storm th' city.

"Thursdah mornin' three thousand full rigimints iv r-rough r-riders swum their hor-rses acrost to Matoonzas, an' afther a spirited battle captured th' Rainy Christiny golf links, two up an' hell to play, an' will hold thim again all comers. Th' same afthernoon th' reg'lar cavalry, con-sistin' iv four hundherd an' eight thousan' well-mounted men, was loaded aboord th' tug Lucy J., and departed on their earned iv death amidst th' cheers iv eight millyon sojers left behind at Chickamaha. These cav'lry'll co-operate with Commodore Schlow; an' whin he desthroys th' Spanish fleet, as he does ivry Sundah an' holy day except in

6

Lent, an' finds out where they ar-re an' desthroys thim, afther
batterin' down th' forts where they ar-re con-cealed so that he
can't see thim, but thinks they ar-re on their way f'r to fight
Cousin George Dooley, th' cav'lry will make a dash back to
Tampa, where Gin'ral Miles is preparin' to desthroy th' Spanish
at wan blow,—an' he's th' boy to blow.

"The gin'ral arrived th' other day, fully prepared f'r th' bloody
wurruk iv war. He had his intire fam'ly with him. He r-rode
recklessly into camp, mounted on a superb specyal ca-ar. As
himsilf an' Uncle Mike Miles, an' Cousin Hennery Miles, an'
Master Miles, aged eight years, dismounted fr'm th' specyal train,
they were received with wild cheers be eight millyon iv th' bravest
sojers that iver give up their lives f'r their counthry. Th' press
cinchorship is so pow'rful that no news is allowed to go out; but
I have it fr'm th' specyal corryspondint iv Mesilf, Clancy th'
Butcher, Mike Casey, an' th' City Direchtry that Gin'ral Miles
instantly repaired himself to th' hotel, where he made his plans
f'r cr-rushin' th' Spanyards at wan blow. He will equip th' ar-
rmy with blow-guns at wanst. His uniforms ar-re comin' down
in specyal steel protected buhyon trains fr'm th' mint, where
they've been kept f'r a year. He has ordhered out th' gold resarve
f'r to equip his staff, numberin' eight thousan' men, manny iv
whom ar-re clubmen; an', as soon as he can have his pitchers
took, he will cr-rush th' Spanish with wan blow. Th' pur-pose iv
th' gin'ral is to permit no delay. Decisive action is demanded be
th' people. An', whin th' hot air masheens has been sint to th'
front, Gin'ral Miles will strike wan blow that'll be th' damdest
blow since th' year iv th' big wind in Ireland.

"Iv coorse, they'se dissinsions in th' cabinet; but they don't
amount to nawthin'. Th' Sicrety iv War is in favor iv sawin' th'
Spanish ar-rmy into two-be-four joists. Th' Sicrety iv th' Threea-
sury has a scheme f'r roonin' thim be lindin' thim money. Th'
Sicrety iv th' Navy wants to sue thim befure th' Mattsachusetts
Supreme Coort. I've heerd that th' Prisident is arrangin' a knee
dhrill, with th' idee iv prayin' th' villyans to th' divvil. But these
diff'rences don't count. We're all wan people, an' we look to
Gin'ral Miles to desthroy th' Spanish with wan blow. Whin it
comes, trees will be lifted out be th' roots. Morro Castle'll cave

in, an' th' air'll be full iv Spanish whiskers. A long blow, a sthrong blow, an' a blow all together."

"We're a gr-reat people," said Mr. Hennessy, earnestly.

"We ar-re," said Mr. Dooley. "We ar-re that. An' th' best iv it is, we know we ar-re."

On Fitz-Hugh Lee

"Iv Coorse, he's Irish," said Mr. Dooley. "Th' Fitz-Hughs an' th' McHughs an' th' McKeoughs is not far apart. I have a cousin be th' name iv McKeough, an' like as not th' gin'ral is a relation iv mine."

"If I was you, I'd write him an' see," said Mr. Hennessy. "He's a gr-reat ma-an."

"He is so," said Mr. Dooley. "He is that. Wan iv th' gr-reatest. An' why shudden't he be with thim two names? They'se pothry in both iv thim. Fitz-Hugh Lee! Did ye iver see a pitcher iv him? A fat ma-an, with a head like a football an' a neck big enough to pump blood into his brain an' keep it fr'm starvin'. White-haired an' r-red-faced. Th' kind iv ma-an that can get mad in ivry vein in his body. Whin he's hot, I bet ye his face looks like a fire in a furniture facthry. Whin a ma-an goes pale with r-rage, look out f'r a knife in th' back. But, whin he flames up so that th' perspi-ration sizzles on his brow, look out f'r hand an' feet an' head an' coupling pins an' rapid-firin' guns. Fitz can be ca'm whin they'se annything to be ca'm about, but he can't wait. If he was a waiter, he'd be wurrukin' at th' thrade. Look at th' jaw iv him! It's like a paving block.

"Does Fitz believe in di-plomacy? Not him. He sets there in his office in Havana, smokin' a good seegar, an' a boy comes in an' tells him they've jugged an American citizen. He jams his hat down on his eyes, an' r-rushes over to where Gin'ral Blanco

9

has his office. 'Look here,' says he, 'ye pizenous riptile,' he says, 'if ye don't have me counthryman out iv th' bull-pen in fifteen minyits be th' watch,' he says, 'I'll take ye be th' hair iv th' head an' pull ye fr'm th' corner iv Halsted Sthreet to th' r-red bridge,' he says. 'Lave us debate this,' says Blanco. 'I'll debate nawthin', says Fitz. 'Hurry up, or I'll give ye a slap,' he says. 'R-run over an' wake up th' loot at th' station, an' let thim Americans out, or,' he says, 'we'll go to the flure,' he says.

"That's Fitz. He's ca'm, an' he waits part iv th' time. That's whin he's asleep. But, as soon as his eyes opins, his face begins to flare up like wan iv thim r-round stoves in a woodman's shanty whin rosiny wood is thrun in. An' fr'm that time on till he's r-ready to tur-rn in an' sleep peaceful an' quite,—not like a lamb full iv vigetable food, but like a line that's wur-rked ha-ard an' et meat,—he niver stops rampin' an' ragin'. Ye don't hear iv Fitz lookin' worn with th' shruggle. Ye don't r-read iv him missin' anny meals. No one fears that Fitz will break down undher th' suspinse. That ain't in th' breed. He's another kind iv a man. He hasn't got th' time to be tired an' worrid. He needs food, an' he has it; an' he needs sleep, an' he takes it; an' he needs fightin', an' he gets it. That's Fitz. They ain't such a lot iv diff'rence between th' bravest man in the wurruld an' th' cow'rdliest. Not such a lot. It ain't a question iv morality, Hinnissy. I've knowed men that wint to church ivry Sundah an' holyday reg'lar, an' give to th' poor an' loved their neighbors, an' they wudden't defind their wives against a murdherer. An' I've knowed th' worst villyuns on earth that'd die in their thracks to save a stranger's child fr'm injury. 'Tis a question iv how th' blood is pumped. Whin a man shows th' sthrain, whin he gets thin an' pale an' worrid in th' time f'r fightin', he's mighty near a cow'rd. But, whin his face flames an' his neck swells an' his eyes look like a couple iv ilicthric lamps again a cyclone sky, he'd lead a forlorn hope acrost th' battlemints iv hell."

On Mules and Others

"I SEE," said Mr. Dooley, "th' first gr-reat land battle iv th' war has been fought."

"Where was that?" demanded Mr. Hennessy, in great excitement. "Lord save us, but where was that?"

"Th' Alger gyards," said Mr. Dooley, "bruk fr'm th' corral where they had thim tied up, atin' thistles, an' med a desp'rate charge on th' camp at Tampa. They dayscinded like a whur-rl-wind, dhrivin' th' astonished throops befure thim, an' thin charged back again, completin' their earned iv desthruction. At th' las' account th' brave sojers was climbin' threes an' tilly-graft poles, an' a rig'mint iv mules was kickin' th' pink silk linin' out iv th' officers' quarthers. Th' gallant mules was led be a most courageous jackass, an' 'tis undhersthud that me frind Mack will appint him a brigadier-gin'ral jus' as soon as he can find out who his father is. 'Tis too bad he'll have no childher to perpituate th' fame iv him. He wint through th' camp at th' head iv his throops iv mules without castin' a shoe. He's th' biggest jackass in Tampa to-day, not exciptin' th' cinsor; an' I doubt if they'se a bigger wan in Wash'n'ton, though I cud name a few that cud thry a race with him. Annyhow, they'll know how to reward him. They know a jackass whin they see wan, an' they see a good manny in that peaceful city.

"Th' charge iv Tampa'll go into histhry as th' first land action iv th' war. An', be th' way, Hinnissy, if this here sociable is f'r

11

to go on at th' prisint rate, I'm sthrong to ar-rm th' wild ar-rmy mules an' the unbridled jackasses iv th' pe-rary an' give thim a chanst to set Cuba free. Up to this time th' on'y hero kilt on th' Spanish side was a jackass that poked an ear above th' batthries at Matoonzas f'r to hear what was goin' on. 'Behold,' says Sampson, 'th' insolince iv th' foe,' he says. 'For-rm in line iv battle, an' hur-rl death an' desthruction at yon Castilyan gin'ral.' 'Wait,' says an officer. 'It may be wan iv our own men. It looks like th' Sicrety iv'—'Hush!' says th' commander. 'It can't be an American jackass, or he'd speak,' he says. 'Fire on him.' Shot afther shot fell round th' inthrepid ass; but he remained firm till th' dinnymite boat Vesoovyus fired three hundherd an' forty thousand pounds iv gum cotton at him, an' the poor crather was smothered to death. Now, says I, give these Tampa mules a chanst, an' we'll have no need iv wastin' ammun-ni-tion. Properly led, they'd go fr'm wan end iv Cuba to th' other, kickin' th' excelsior out iv ivry stuffed Spanish gin'ral fr'm Bahoohoo Hoondoo to Sandago de Cuba. They'd be no loss iv life. Th' sojers who haven't gone away cud come home an' get cured iv th' measles an' th' whoopin'-cough an' th' cholera infantum befure th' public schools opens in th' fall, an' iverything wud be peaceful an' quiet an' prosp'rous. Th' officers in th' field at prisint is well qualified f'r command iv th' new ar-rmy; an', if they'd put blinders on th' mules, they wudden't be scared back be wan iv thim Spanish fleets that a jackass sees whin he's been up all night, secretly stuffing himsilf with silo. They'd give wan hewhaw, an' follow their leaders through th' hear-rt iv th' inimy's counthry. But give thim th' wurrud to git ap, an' they'd ate their thistles undher th' guns iv some ol' Morrow Castle befure night.

"Ye don't see th' diff'rence, says ye. They ain't anny i' th' leaders. As efficient a lot iv mules as iver exposed their ears. Th' throuble is with th' rank an' file. They're men. What's needed to carry on this war as it goes to-day is an ar-rmy iv jacks an' mules. Whin ye say to a man, 'Git ap, whoa, gee, back up, get alang!' he don't know what ye'er dhrivin' at or to. But a mule hears th' ordhers with a melancholy smile, dhroops his ears, an' follows his war-rm, moist breath. Th' ordhers fr'm Washin'ton is perfectly comprehinsible to a jackasss, but they don't mane annything to a poor, foolish man. No human bein',

Hinnissy, can undherstand what the divvle use it was to sink a ship that cost two hundherd thousan' dollars an' was worth at laste eighty dollars in Sandago Harbor, if we have to keep four-teen ships outside to prevint five Spanish ships fr'm sailin'. Th' poor, tired human mind don't tumble, Hinnissy, to th' raison f'r landin' four hundherd marines at Guanotommy to clear th' forests, whin Havanna is livin' free on hot tamales an' icecream. Th' mind iv a Demostheens or a Tim Hogan would be crippled thryin' to figure out why throops ar-re sint out fr'm Tampa an' thin ordhered back through a speakin' chube, while wan iv th' new briga-deer-gin'rals has his hands manicured an' says good-by to his nurse. But it ought to be as plain to th' mule that hears it as it is to th' jackasses that gets it up. What we need, Hinnissy, is a perfect undherstandin' between th' ar-rmy an' th' admin-isthration. We need what Hogan calls th' esphrite th' corpse, an' we'll on'y have it whin th' mules begins to move."

"I shud think," said Mr. Hennessy, "now that th' jackasses has begun to be onaisy" —

"We ought to be afraid th' cabinet an' th' Boord iv Sthrateejy'll be stampeded?" Mr. Dooley interrupted. "Niver fear. They're too near th' fodder."

13

On His Cousin George

"WELL," said Mr. Hennessy, in tones of chastened joy: "Dewey didn't do a thing to thim. I hope th' poor la-ad ain't cooped up there in Minneapolis."

"Niver fear," said Mr. Dooley, calmly. "Cousin George is all r-right."

"Cousin George?" Mr. Hennessy exclaimed.

"Sure," said Mr. Dooley. "Dewey or Dooley, 'tis all th' same. We dhrop a letter here an' there, except th' haitches, — we niver dhrop thim, — but we're th' same breed iv fightin' men. Georgy has th' thraits iv th' fam'ly. Me uncle Mike, that was a handy man, was tol' wanst he'd be sint to hell f'r his manny sins, an' he desarved it; f'r, lavin' out th' wan sin iv runnin' away fr'm annywan, he was booked f'r ivrything from murdher to missin' mass. 'Well,' he says, 'anny place I can get into,' he says, 'I can get out iv,' he says. 'Ye bet on that,' he says.

"So it is with Cousin George. He knew th' way in, an' it's th' same way out. He didn't go in be th' fam'ly inthrance, sneakin' along with th' can undher his coat. He left Ding Dong, or what- iver 'tis ye call it, an' says he, 'Thank Gawd,' he says, 'I'm where no man can give me his idees iv how to r-run quiltin' party, an' call it war,' he says. An' so he sint a man down in a divin' shute, an' cut th' cables, so's Mack cudden't chat with him. Thin he prances up to th' Spanish forts, an' hands thim a few oranges. Tosses thim out like a man throwin' handbills f'r a circus. 'Take

14

that,' he says, 'an' raymimber th' Maine,' he says. An' he goes into th' harbor, where Admiral What-th'-'ell is, an', says he, 'Surrinder,' he says. 'Niver,' says th' Dago. 'Well,' says Cousin George, 'I'll just have to push ye ar-round,' he says. An' he tosses a few slugs at th' Spanyards. Th' Spanish admiral shoots at him with a bow an' arrow, an' goes over an' writes a cable. 'This mornin' we was attackted,' he says. 'An,' he says, 'we fought the inimy with great courage,' he says. 'Our victhry is com-plete,' he says. 'We have lost ivrything we had,' he says. 'Th' threachrous foe,' he says, 'afther destroyin' us, sought refuge behind a mud-scow,' he says; 'but nawthin' daunted us. What boats we cudden't r-run ashore we surrindered,' he says. 'I cannot write no more,' he says, 'as me coat-tails are afire,' he says; 'an' I am bravely but rapidly leapin' fr'm wan vessel to another, followed be me valiant crew with a fire-engine,' he says. 'If I can save me coat-tails,' he says, 'they'll be no kick comin',' he says. 'Long live Spain, long live mesilf.'

"Well, sir, in twenty-eight minyits be th' clock Dewey he had all th' Spanish boats sunk, an' that there harbor lookin' like a Spanish stew. Thin he r-run down th' bay, an' handed a few war-rm wans into th' town. He set it on fire, an' wint ashore to war-rm his poor hands an' feet. It chills th' blood not to have an-nything to do f'r an hour or more."

"Thin why don't he write something?" Mr. Hennessy de-manded.

"Write?" echoed Mr. Dooley. "Write? Why shud he write? D'ye think Cousin George ain't got nawthin' to do but to set down with a fountain pen, an' write: 'Dear Mack, — At 8 o'clock I begun a peaceful blockade iv this town. Ye can see th' pieces ivrywhere. I hope ye're injyin' th' same gr-reat blessin'. So no more at prisint. Fr'm ye'ers thruly, George Dooley.' He ain't that kind. 'Tis a nice day, an' he's there smokin' a good tin-cint see-gar, an' thrownin' dice f'r th' dhrinks. He don't care whether we know what he's done or not. I'll bet ye, whin we come to find out about him, we'll hear he's ilicted himself king iv th' F'lip-ine Islands. Dooley th' Wanst. He'll be settin' up there undher a pa'm-three with naygurs fannin' him an' a dhrop iv licker in th' hollow iv his ar-rm, an' hootchy-kootchy girls dancin' befure him, an' ivry tin or twinty minyits some wan bringin' a prisoner in. 'Who's this?' says King Dooley. 'A Spanish gin'ral,' says th' copper. 'Give him a typewriter an' set him to wurruk,' says th' king. 'On with th' dance,' he says. An' afther awhile, whin he gits tired iv th' game, he'll write home an' say he's got the islands; an' he'll tur-rn thim over to th' gover'mint an' go back to his ship, an' Mark Hanna'll organize th' F'lip-ine Islands Jute an' Cider Comp'ny, an' th' rivolutchinists'll wish they hadn't. That's what'll happen. Mark me wurrud."

On Some Army Appointments

"WELL, sir," said Mr. Dooley, "I didn't vote f'r Mack, but I'm with him now. I had me doubts whether he was th' gr-reatest military janius iv th' cinchry, but they'se no question about it. We go into this war, if we iver do go into it, with th' most fash'nable ar-rmy that iver creased its pants. 'Twill be a daily hint fr'm Paris to th' crool foe.

"Other gin'rals iv th' r-rough-house kind, like Napoleon Bonypart, th' impror iv th' Frinch, Gin'ral Ulis S. Grant, an' Cousin George Dooley, hired coarse, rude men that wudden't know th' diff'rence between goluf an' crokay, an' had their pants tucked in their boots an' chewed tobacco be th' pound. Thank Hivin, McKinley knows betther thin to sind th' likes iv thim abroad to shock our frinds be dumpin' their coffee into thimsilves fr'm a saucer.

"Th' dure bell rings, an' a futman in liv'ry says: 'I'm Master Willie Dooselbery's man, an' he's come to be examined f'r th' army,' says he. 'Admit him,' says McKinley; an' Master Willie enters, accompanied be his val-lay, his mah an' pah an' th' comity iv th' goluf club. 'Willie,' says th' Prisident, 'ye ar-re enthrin' upon a gloryous car-eer, an' 'tis nic'ssry that ye shud be thurly examined, so that ye can teach th' glories iv civilization to th' tyr-ranies iv Europe that is supported be ye'er pah an' mah,' he says. 'Twud be a turr'ble thing,' he says, 'if some day they shud meet a Spanish gin'ral in Mahdrid, an' have him say to thim, "I

17

seen ye'er son Willie durin' th' war wearin' a stovepipe hat an'
tan shoes." Let us begin th' examination,' he says. 'Ar-re ye a
good goluf player?' 'I am,' says Willie. 'Thin I appint ye a liftnant.
What we need in th' ar-rmy is good goluf players,' he says. 'In
our former war,' he says, 'we had th' misfortune to have men
in command that didn't know th' diff'rence between a goluf
stick an' a beecycle; an' what was th' raysult? We foozled our
approach at Bull R-run,' he says. 'Ar-re ye a mimber iv anny
clubs?' he says. 'Four,' says Willie. 'Thin I make ye a major,' he
says. 'Where d'ye get ye'er pants?' he says. 'Fr'm England,' says
Willie. 'Gloryous,' says McKinley. 'I make ye a colonel,' he says.
'Let me thry ye in tactics,' he says. 'Suppose ye was confronted
be a Spanish ar-rmy in th' afthernoon, how wud ye dhress?' he
says. 'I'd wear a stovepipe hat, a long coat, a white vest, an'
lavendar pants,' says Willie. 'An' if th' attack was be night?' he
says. 'I'd put on me dhress shoot, an' go out to meet thim,' says
Willie. 'A thuro sojer,' says McKinley. 'Suppose th' sociable lasted
all night?' he says. 'I'd sound th' rethreat at daybreak, an' have
me brave boys change back,' he says, 'to suitable appar'l,' he
says. 'Masterly,' says McKinley. 'I will sind ye'er name in as a
brigadier-gin'ral,' he says. 'Thank Gawd, th' r-rich,' he says, 'is
brave an' pathriotic,' he says. 'Ye will jine th' other boys fr'm
th' club at Tampa,' he says. 'Ye shud be careful iv ye'er equip-
ment,' he says. 'I have almost ivrything r-ready,' says Willie. 'Me
man attinded to thim details,' he says. 'But I fear I can't go to
th' fr-ront immejetly,' he says. 'Me pink silk pijammas hasn't
arrived,' he says. 'Well,' says Mack, 'wait f'r thim,' he says. 'I'm
anxious f'r to ind this hor'ble war,' he says, 'which has cost me
manny a sleepy night,' he says; 'but 'twud be a crime f'r to sind
a sojer onprepared to battle,' he says. 'Wait f'r th' pijammas,' he
says. 'Thin on to war,' he says; 'an' let ye'er watchword be,
"Raymimber ye'er manners," ' he says.

" 'They'se a man out here,' says th' privit sicrity, 'that wants
to see ye,' he says. 'He's a r-rough-lookin' charackter that was
in th' Soo war,' he says. 'His name is Gin'ral Fiteum,' he says.
'Throw th' stiff out,' says Mack. 'I seen him in Pinnsylvania Avnoo
yisterdah, r-ridin' in a sthreet ca-ar,' he says. 'Ah, Willie, me boy,'
he says, ''tis little ye know what throuble I have fr'm these vulgar
sojers with pants that bags at th' knees. Give me a goold-tipped

cigareet, an' tell me whether shirt waists is much worn in New York this year.'

"Yis, Hinnissy, we'll put th' tastiest ar-rmy in th' field that iver come out iv a millinery shop. 'Right dhress!' will be an ordher that'll mean somethin'. Th' ar-rmy'll be followed be specyal correspondints fr'm Butthrick's Pattherns an' Harper's Bazar; an', if our brave boys don't gore an' pleat th' inimy, 'twill be because th' inimy'll be r-rude enough to shoot in anny kind iv clothes they find on th' chair whin they wake up."

On Strategy

"A STHRATEEJAN," said Mr. Dooley, in response to Mr. Hennessy's request for information, "is a champeen checker-player. Whin th' war broke out, me frind Mack wint to me frind Hanna, an' says he, 'What,' he says, 'what can we do to cr-rush th' haughty power iv Spain,' he says, 'a'n br-ring this hateful war to a early conclusion?'" he says. 'Mobilize th' checker-players,' says Hanna. An' fr'm all cor-rners iv th' counthry they've gone to Washin'ton, where they're called th' Sthrateejy Board.

"Day an' night they set in a room with a checker-board on th' end iv a flour bar'l, an' study problems iv th' navy. At night Mack dhrops in. 'Well, boys,' says he, 'how goes th' battle?' he says. 'Gloryous,' says th' Sthrateejy Board. 'Two more moves, an' we'll be in th' king row.' 'Ah,' says Mack, 'this is too good to be thrue,' he says. 'In but a few brief minyits th' dhrinks'll be on Spain,' he says. 'Have ye anny plans f'r Sampson's fleet?' he says. 'Where is it?' says th' Sthrateejy Board. 'I dinnaw,' says Mack. 'Good,' says th' Sthrateejy Board. 'Where's th' Spanish fleet?' says they. 'Bombardin' Boston, at Cadiz, in San June de Matzoon, sighted near th' gashouse be our special correspondint, copyright, 1898, be Mike O'Toole.' 'A sthrong position,' says th' Sthrateejy Board. 'Undoubtedly, th' fleet is headed south to attack and seize Armour's glue facthory. Ordher Sampson to sail north as fast as he can, an' lay in a supply iv ice. Th' summer's comin' on. Insthruct Schley to put on all steam, an' thin put it off again, an' call us up be telephone. R-rush eighty-three millyon throops an' four mules to Tampa, to Mobile, to Chickenmaha, to Coney Island, to Ireland, to th' divvle, an' r-rush thim back again. Don't r-rush thim. Ordher Sampson to pick up th' cable at Lincoln Par-rk, an' run into th' bar-rn. Is th' balloon corpse r-ready? It is? Thin don't sind it up. Sind it up. Have th' Mulligan Gyards co-op'rate with Gomez, an' tell him to cut away his whiskers. They've got tangled in th' riggin'. We need yellow-fever throops. Have ye anny yellow fever in th' house? Give it to twinty thousand three hundherd men, an' sind thim afther Gov'nor Tanner. Teddy Rosenfelt's r-rough r-riders ar-re down-stairs, havin' their uniforms pressed. Ordher thim to th' goluf links at wanst. They must be no indecision. Where's Richard Harding Davis? Oh th' bridge iv the New York? Tur-rn th' bridge. Seize Gin'ral Miles' uniform. We must strengthen th' gold re-sarve. Where's th' Gussie? Runnin' off to Cuba with wan hun-dherd men an' ar-rms, iv coorse. Oh, war is a dhreadful thing. It's ye'er move, Claude,' says th' Sthrateejy Board.

"An' so it goes on; an' day by day we r-read th' tur-rble story iv our brave sthrateejans sacrificin' their time on th' altar iv their counthry, as Hogan says. Little we thought, whin we wint into this war, iv th' horrors it wud bring. Little we thought iv th' mothers at home weepin' f'r their brave boys down at Washin'ton hur-rtin their poor eyes over a checker-board. Little we thought iv these devoted men, as Hogan says, with achin' heads, plannin' to sind three hundherd thousand millyon men an' a carload iv beans to their fate at Tampa, Fla. But some wan must be sac-rificed, as Hogan says. An' these poor fellows in Washin'ton with their r-red eyes an' their tired backs will be an example to future ginerations, as Hogan says, iv how an American sojer can face his jooty whin he has to, an' how he can't whin he hasn't to."

"Dewey ain't a sthrateejan?" inquired Mr. Hennessy.

"No," said Mr. Dooley. "Cousin George is a good man, an' I'm very fond iv him,—more be raison iv his doin' that May-o bosthoon Pat Mountjoy, but he has low tastes. We niver cud make a sthrateejan iv him. They'se a kind iv a vulgar fightin' sthrain in him that makes him want to go out an' slug some wan wanst a month. I'm glad he ain't in Washin'ton. Th' chances ar-re he'd go to th' Sthrateejy Board and pull its hair."

On General Miles's Moonlight Excursion

"DEAR, oh, dear," said Mr. Dooley, "I'd give five dollars—an' I'd kill a man f'r three—if I was out iv this Sixth Wa-ard to-night, an' down with Gin'ral Miles' gran' picnic an' moonlight excursion in Porther Ricky. 'Tis no comfort in bein' a cow'rd whin ye think iv thim br-rave la-ads facin' death be suffication in bokays an' dyin' iv waltzin' with th' pretty girls iv Porther Ricky.

"I dinnaw whether Gin'ral Miles picked out th' job or whether 'twas picked out f'r him. But, annyhow, whin he got to Sandago de Cubia an' looked ar-round him, he says to his frind Gin'ral Shafter, 'Gin'ral,' says he, 'ye have done well so far,' he says. ''Tis not f'r me to take th' lorls fr'm th' steamin' brow iv a thrue hero,' he says. 'I lave ye here,' he says, 'f'r to complete th' victhry ye have so nobly begun,' he says. 'F'r you,' he says, 'th' wallop in th' eye fr'm th' newspaper rayporther, th' r-round robbing, an' th' sunsthroke,' he says, 'f'r me th' hardship iv th' battlefield, th' late dinner, th' theayter party, an' th' sickenin' polky,' he says. 'Gather,' he says, 'th' fruits iv ye'er bravery,' he says. 'Return,' he says, 'to ye'er native land, an' receive anny gratichood th' Sicrety iv War can spare fr'm his own fam'ly,' he says. 'F'r me,' he says, 'there is no way but f'r to tur-rn me back upon this festive scene,' he says, 'an' go where jooty calls me,' he says. 'Ordherly,' he says, 'put a bottle on th' ice, an' see that me goold pants that I wear with th' pale blue vest with th' di'mon buttons is irned out,' he says. An' with a haggard face he walked aboord th' excursion steamer, an' wint away.

"I'd hate to tell ye iv th' thriles iv th' expedition, Hinnissy. Whin th' picnic got as far as Punch, on th' southern coast iv Porther Ricky, Gin'ral Miles gazes out, an' says he, 'This looks like a good place to hang th' hammicks, an' have lunch,' says he. 'Forward, brave men,' says he, 'where ye see me di'mon's sparkle,' says he. 'Forward, an' plant th' crokay ar-rches iv our beloved counthry,' he says. An' in they wint, like inthrepid war-ryors that they ar-re. On th' beach they was met be a diligation fr'm th' town of Punch, con-sistin' iv th' mayor, th' common council, th' polis an' fire departments, th' Gr-rand Ar-rmy iv th' Raypublic, an' prominent citizens in carredges. Gin'ral Miles, makin' a hasty tielet, advanced onflinchingly to meet them. 'Gin-tlemen,' says he, 'what can I do f'r ye?' he says. 'We come,' says th' chairman iv th' comity, 'f'r to offer ye,' he says, 'th' r-run iv th' town,' he says. 'We have held out,' he says, 'as long as we cud,' he says. 'But,' he says, 'they'se a limit to human endurance,' he says. 'We can withstand ye no longer,' he says. 'We surrinder. Take us prisoners, an' rayceive us into ye'er gloryous an' well-fed raypublic,' he says. 'Br-rave men,' says Gin'ral Miles, 'I con-gratulate ye,' he says, 'on th' heeroism iv yer definse,' he says. 'Ye stuck manfully to yer colors, whativer they ar-re,' he says. 'I on'y wondher that ye waited f'r me to come befure surrindhrin',' he says. 'I welcome ye into th' Union,' he says. 'I don't know how th' Union'll feel about it, but that's no business iv mine,' he says. 'Ye will get ye'er wur-rkin-cards fr'm th' walkin' diligate,' he says; 'an' ye'll be entitled,' he says, 'to pay ye'er share iv th' taxes an' to live awhile an' die whin ye get r-ready,' he says, 'jus' th' same as if ye was bor-rn at home,' he says. 'I don't know th' names iv ye; but I'll call ye all Casey, f'r short,' he says. 'Put ye'er bokays in th' hammick,' he says, 'an' return to Punch,' he says; 'an' freeze somethin' f'r me,' he says, 'f'r me thrawt is parched with th' labors iv th' day,' he says. Th' r-rest iv th' avenin' was spint in dancin', music, an' boat-r-ridin'; an' an inj'-yable time was had.

"Th' nex' day th' army moved on Punch; an' Gin'ral Miles marched into th' ill-fated city, preceded be flower-girls sthrewin' r-roses an' geranyums befure him. In th' afthernoon they was a lawn tinnis party, an' at night the gin'ral attinded a banket at th' Gran' Palace Hotel. At midnight he was serenaded be th' Raymimber th' Maine Banjo an' Mandolin Club. Th' entire popylace attinded, with pork chops in their buttonholes to show their pathreetism. Th' nex' day, afther breakfastin' with Mayor Casey, he set out on his weary march over th' r-rough, flower-strewn paths f'r San Joon. He has been in gr-reat purl fr'm a witherin' fire iv bokays, an' he has met an' overpowered some iv th' mos' savage orators in Porther Ricky; but, whin I las' heerd iv him, he had pitched his tents an' ice-cream freezers near the inimy's wall, an' was grajully silencin' thim with proclamations."

"They'll kill him with kindness if he don't look out," said Mr. Hennessy.

"I dinnaw about that," said Mr. Dooley; "but I know this, that there's th' makin' iv gr-reat statesmen in Porther Ricky. A proud people that can switch as quick as thim la-ads have nawthin' to larn in th' way iv what Hogan calls th' signs iv gover'mint, even fr'm th' Supreme Court."

On Admiral Dewey's Activity

"If they don't catch up with him pretty soon," said Mr. Dooley, "he'll fight his way ar-round th' wurruld, an' come out through Bar-saloona or Cades."

"Who's that?" asked Mr. Hennessy.

"Me Cousin George, no less," said Mr. Dooley. "I suppose ye think th' war is over an' peace has rayturned jus' because Tiddy Rosenfelt is back home again an' th' sojers ar-re hungry in New York 'stead iv in Sandago. That's where ye'er wrong, Hinnissy. That's where ye'er wrong, me bucko. Th' war is not over till Cousin George stops fightin'. Th' Spanyards have had enough, but among thrue fightin' men it don't make anny diff'rence what th' feelin's iv th' la-ad undherneath may be. 'Tis whin th' man on top has had his fill iv fightin' that th' throuble's over, an' be the look iv things Cousin George has jus' begun to take tay.

"Whin me frind Mack con-cluded 'twas time f'r us to stop fightin' an' begin skinning each other in what Hogan calls th' marts iv thrade, ye thought that ended it. So did Mack. He says, says he, 'Let us have peace,' he says. An' Mark Hanna came out iv' th' cellar, where he's been since Cousin George presinted his compliments to th' Ph'lippines an' wud they prefer to be kilt or dhrownded, an' pro-posals was made to bond th' Cubian path-rites, an' all th' deuces in th' deck begun to look like face car-rds again, whin suddenly there comes a message fr'm Cousin George. 'In pursooance iv ordhers that niver come,' he says, 'to-day th' squadhron undher my command knocked th' divvle out iv th' fortifications iv th' Ph'lippines, bombarded the city, an' locked up th' insurgent gin'ral. The gov'nor got away be swimmin' aboord a Dutch ship, an' th' Dutchman took him to Ding Dong. I'll attind to th' Dutchman some afthernoon whin I have nawthin' else to do. I'm settin' in the palace with me feet on th' pianny. Write soon. I won't get it. So no more at prisint, fr'm ye'er ol' frind an' well-wisher, George Dooley.'

"How ar-re they goin' to stop him? How ar-re they goin' to stop him? There's Mack on th' shore bawlin' ordhers. 'Come back,' he says. 'Come back, I com-mand ye,' he says. 'George, come back,' he says. 'Th' war is over,' he says. 'We're at peace with th' wurruld,' he says. 'George,' he says, 'George, be a good fellow,' he says. 'Lave up on thim,' he says. 'Hivins an' earth, he's batin' that poor Spanyard with a pavin' block. George, George, ye break me hear-rt,' he says.

"But George Dooley, he gives th' wink to his frinds, an' says he, 'What's that man yellin' on th' shore about?' he says. 'Louder,' he says. 'I can't hear ye,' he says. 'Sing it,' he says. 'Write it to me on a postal ca-ard at Mahdrid,' he says. 'Don't stop me now,' he says. 'This is me, busy day,' he says; an' away he goes with a piece iv lead pipe in wan hand an' a couplin' pin in th' other.

"What'll we do with him? We can't catch up with him. He's goin' too fast. Mack's a week behind him ivry time he stops annywhere. He has sthrung a throlley acrost th' islands, an' he's climbin' mountains with his fleet. Th' on'y thing I see, Hinnissy, that Mack can do is to go east an' meet him comin' r-round. If he hurries, he'll sthrike him somewhere in Rooshia or Boohl-gahria, an' say to him: 'George, th' war's over. Won't ye come home with me?' I think he'll listen to reason."

"I think a man ought to stop fightin' whin th' war is ended," said Mr. Hennessy.

"I dinnaw about that," said Mr. Dooley. "He started without askin' our lave, an' I don't see what we've got to do with th' way he finishes. 'Tis a tur-rble thing to be a man iv high sperrits, an' not to know whin th' other fellow's licked."

26

On the Philippines

"I KNOW what I'd do if I was Mack," said Mr. Hennessy. "I'd hist a flag over th' Ph'lippeens, an' I'd take in th' whole lot iv thim."

"An' yet," said Mr. Dooley, "tis not more thin two months since ye larned whether they were islands or canned goods. Ye'er back yard is so small that ye'er cow can't turn r-round without buttin' th' woodshed off th' premises, an' ye wudden't go out to th' stock yards without takin' out a policy on yer life. Suppose ye was standin' at th' corner iv State Sthreet an' Archey R-road, wud ye know what car to take to get to th' Ph'lippeens? If yer son Packy was to ask ye where th' Ph'lippeens is, cud ye give him anny good idea whether they was in Rooshia or jus' west iv th' thracks?"

"Mebbe I cudden't," said Mr. Hennessy, haughtily, "but I'm f'r takin' thim in, annyhow."

"So might I be," said Mr. Dooley, "if I cud on'y get me mind on it. Wan iv the worst things about this here war is th' way it's makin' puzzles f'r our poor, tired heads. Whin I wint into it, I thought all I'd have to do was to set up here behind th' bar with a good tin-cint see-gar in me teeth, an' toss dinnymite bombs into th' hated city iv Havanna. But look at me now. Th' war is still goin' on; an' ivry night, whin I'm countin' up the cash, I'm askin' mesilf will I annex Cubia or lave it to the Cubians? Will I take Porther Ricky or put it by? An' what shud I do with the

27

Ph'lippeens? Oh, what shud I do with thim? I can't annex thim because I don't know where they ar-re. I can't let go iv thim because some wan else'll take thim if I do. They are eight thousan' iv thim islands, with a popylation iv wan hundherd millyon naked savages; an' me bedroom's crowded now with me an' th' bed. How can I take thim in, an' how on earth am I goin' to cover th' nakedness iv thim savages with me wan shoot iv clothes? An' yet 'twud break me heart to think iv givin' people I niver see or heerd tell iv back to other people I don't know. An', if I don't take thim, Schwartzmeister down th' sthreet, that has half me thrade already, will grab thim sure.

"It ain't that I'm afraid iv not doin' th' r-right thing in th' end, Hinnissy. Some mornin' I'll wake up an' know jus' what to do, an' that I'll do. But 'tis th' annoyance in th' mane time. I've been r-readin' about th' counthry. 'Tis over beyant ye'er left shoulder whin ye're facin' east. Jus' throw ye'er thumb back, an' ye have it as ac'rate as anny man in town. 'Tis farther thin Boohlgahrya an' not so far as Blewchoochoo. It's near Chiny, an' it's not so near; an', if a man was to bore a well through fr'm Goshen, Indianny, he might sthrike it, an' thin again he might not. It's a poverty-sthricken counthry, full iv goold an' precious stones, where th' people can pick dinner off th' threes an' ar-re starvin' because they have no stepladders. Th' inhabitants is mostly naygurs an' Chinnymen, peaceful, industhrus, an' law-abidin', but savage an' bloodthirsty in their methods. They wear no clothes except what they have on, an' each woman has five husbands an' each man has five wives. Th' r-rest goes into th' discard, th' same as here. Th' islands has been ownded be Spain since befure th' fire; an' she's threated thim so well they're now up in ar-rms again her, except a majority iv thim which is thurly loyal. Th' natives seldom fight, but whin they get mad at wan another they r-run-a-muck. Whin a man r-runs-a-muck, sometimes they hang him an' sometimes they discharge him an' hire a new motorman. Th' women ar-re beautiful, with languishin' black eyes, an' they smoke see-gars, but ar-re hurried an' incomplete in their dhress. I see a pitcher iv wan th' other day with nawthin' on her but a basket of cocoanuts an' a hoopskirt. They're no prudes. We import juke, hemp, cigar wrappers, sugar, an' fairy tales fr'm th' Ph'lippeens, an' export six-inch shells an' th' like. Iv late th' Ph'lippeens has awaked to th' fact that they're behind th' times, an' has received much American amminition in their midst. They say th' Spanyards is all tore up about it.

"I larned all this fr'm th' papers, an' I know 'tis sthraight. An' yet, Hinnissy, I dinnaw what to do about th' Ph'lippeens. An' I'm all alone in th' wurruld. Ivrybody else has made up his mind. Ye ask anny con-ducthor on Ar-rchy R-road, an' he'll tell ye. Ye can find out fr'm the papers; an', if ye really want to know, all ye have to do is to ask a prom'nent citizen who can mow all th' lawn he owns with a safety razor. But I don't know."

"Hang on to thim," said Mr. Hennessy, stoutly. "What we've got we must hold."

"Well," said Mr. Dooley, "if I was Mack, I'd lave it to George. I'd say: 'George,' I'd say, 'if ye're f'r hangin' on, hang on it is. If ye say, lave go, I dhrop thim.' 'Twas George won thim with th' shells, an' th' question's up to him."

On Prayers for Victory

"IT looks to me," said Mr. Dooley, "as though me frind Mack'd got tired iv th' Sthrateejy Board, an' was goin' to lave th' war to th' men in black."

"How's that?" asked Mr. Hennessy, who has at best but a clouded view of public affairs.

"Well," said Mr. Dooley, "while th' sthrateejans have been wearin' out their jeans on cracker-boxes in Wash'n'ton, they'se been goin' on th' mos' deadly conflict iver heerd tell iv between th' pow'rful preachin' navies iv th' two counthries. Manila is nawthin' at all to th' scenes iv carnage an' slaughter, as Hogan says, that's been brought about be these desthroyers. Th' Spanyards fired th' openin' gun whin th' bishop iv Cades, a pow'rful turreted monitor (ol' style), attackted us with both for'ard guns, an' sint a storm iv brimstone an' hell into us. But th' victhry was not f'r long with th' hated Spanyard. He was answered be our whole fleet iv preachers. Thin he was jined be th' bishop iv Barsaloona an' th' bishop iv Mahdrid an' th' bishop iv Havana, all battle-ships iv th' first class, followed be a fleet iv cruisers r-runnin' all th' way fr'm a full-ar-rmored vicar gin'ral to a protected parish priest. To meet thim, we sint th' bishop iv New York, th' bishop iv Philadelphia, th' bishop iv Baltimore, an' th' bishop iv Chicago, accompanied be a flyin' squadhron iv Methodists, three Presbyteryan monitors, a fleet iv Baptist submarine desthroyers, an' a formidable array iv Universalist an' Unitaryan torpedo boats, with a Jew r-ram. Manetime th' bishop iv Manila had fired a solid prayer, weighin' a ton, at San Francisco; an' a masked batthry iv Congregationalists replied, inflictin' severe damage. Our Atlantic fleet is now sarchin' f'r th' inimy, an' the bishop iv New York is blockadin' th' bishop iv Sandago de Cuba; an' they'se been an exchange iv prayers between th' bishop iv Baltimore an' th' bishop iv Havana without much damage.

"Th' Lord knows how it'll come out. First wan side prays that th' wrath iv Hiven'll descind on th' other, an' thin th' other side returns th' compliment with inthrest. Th' Spanish bishop says we're a lot iv murdherin', irreligious thieves, an' ought to be swept fr'm th' face iv th' earth. We say his people ar-re th' same, an' manny iv thim. He wishes Hivin to sink our ships an' desthroy our men; an' we hope he'll injye th' same gr-reat blessin'. We have a shade th' best iv him, f'r his fleets ar-re all iv th' same class an' ol' style, an' we have some iv th' most modhern prayin' machines in the warruld; but he prays har-rd, an' 'tis no aisy wurruk to silence him."

"What d'ye think about it?" asked Mr. Hennessy.

"Well," said Mr. Dooley, "I dinnaw jus' what to think iv it. Me own idee is that war is not a matther iv prayers so much as a matther iv punchin'; an' th' on'y place a prayer book stops a bullet is in th' story books. 'Tis like what Father Kelly said. Three weeks ago las' Sundah he met Hogan; an' Hogan, wantin' to be smart, ast him if he'd offered up prayers f'r th' success iv th' cause. 'Faith, I did not,' says th' good man. 'I was in too much iv a hurry to get away.' 'What was th' matther?' ast Hogan. 'I had me uniform to brush up an' me soord to polish,' says Father Kelly. 'I am goin' with th' rig'mint to-morrah,' he says; an' he says, 'If ye hear iv me waitin' to pray,' he says, 'anny time they'se a call f'r me,' he says, 'to be in a fight,' he says, 'ye may conclude,' he says, 'that I've lost me mind, an' won't be back to me parish,' he says. 'Hogan,' he says, 'I'll go into th' battle with a prayer book in wan hand an' a soord in th' other,' he says; 'an', if th' wurruk calls f'r two hands, 'tis not th' soord I'll dhrop,' he says. 'Don't ye believe in prayer?' says Hogan. 'I do,' says th' good man; 'but,' he says, 'a healthy person ought,' he says, 'to be ashamed,' he says, 'to ask f'r help in a fight,' he says."

"That's th' way I look at it," said Mr. Hennessy. "When 'tis an aven thing in th' prayin', may th' best man win."

"Ye're r-right, Hinnissy," said Mr. Dooley, warmly. "Ye're r-right. An' th' best man will win."

On the Anglo-Saxon

"Well," said Mr. Dooley, "I see be th' pa-apers that th' snow-white pigeon iv peace have tied up th' dogs iv war. It's all over now. All we've got to do is to arrest th' pathrites an' make th' reconcenthradios pay th' stamp tax, an' be r-ready f'r to take a punch at Germany or France or Rooshia or anny counthry on th' face iv th' globe.

"An' I'm glad iv it. This war, Hinnissy, has been a gr-reat sthrain on me. To think iv th' suffrin' I've endured! F'r weeks I lay awake at nights fearin' that th' Spanish ar-rmadillo'd lave the Cape Verde Islands, where it wasn't, an' take th' thrain out here, an' hur-rl death an' desthruction into me little store. Day be day th' pitiless exthries come out an' beat down on me. Ye hear iv Teddy Rosenfelt plungin' into ambus-cades an' Sicrity iv Wars; but d'ye hear iv Martin Dooley, th' man behind th' guns, four thousan' miles behind thim, an' willin' to be further? They ar-re no bokays f'r me. I'm what Hogan calls wan iv th' mute, inglory-ous heroes iv th' war; an' not so dam mute, ayther. Some day, Hinnissy, justice'll be done me, an' th' likes iv me; an', whin th' story iv a gr-reat battle is written, they'll print th' kilt, th' wounded, th' missin', an' th' seryously disturbed. An' thim that have bore thimsilves well an' bravely an' paid th' taxes an' faced th' deadly newspa-apers without flinchin' 'll be advanced six pints an' given a chanst to tur-rn jack f'r th' game.

33

"But me wurruk ain't over jus' because Mack has inded th' war an' Teddy Rosenfelt is comin' home to bite th' Sicrety iv War. You an' me, Hinnissy, has got to bring on this here Anglo-Saxon 'lieance. An Anglo-Saxon, Hinnissy, is a German that's forgot who was his parents. They're a lot iv thim in this counthry. There must be as manny as two in Boston: they'se wan up in Maine, an' another lives at Bogg's Ferry in New York State, an' dhrives a milk wagon. Mack is an Anglo-Saxon. His folks come fr'm th' County Armagh, an' their naytional Anglo-Saxon hymn is 'O'Donnell Aboo.' Teddy Rosenfelt is another Anglo-Saxon. An' I'm an Anglo-Saxon. I'm wan iv th' hottest Anglo-Saxons that iver come out iv Anglo-Saxony. Th' name iv Dooley has been th' proudest Anglo-Saxon name in th' County Roscommon f'r many years.

"Schwartzmeister is an Anglo-Saxon, but he doesn't know it, an' won't till some wan tells him. Pether Bowbeen down be th' Frinch church is formin' th' Circle Francaize Anglo-Saxon club, an' me ol' frind Dominigo that used to boss th' Ar-rchey R-road wagon whin Callaghan had th' sthreet conthract will march at th' head iv th' Dago Anglo-Saxons whin th' time comes. There ar-re twinty thousan' Rooshian Jews at a quarther a vote in th' Sivinth Ward; an', ar-rmed with rag hooks, they'd be a tur-r-ble thing f'r anny inimy iv th' Anglo-Saxon 'lieance to face. Th' Bohemians an' Pole Anglo-Saxons may be a little slow in wakin' up to what th' pa-apers calls our common hurtage, but ye may be sure they'll be all r-right whin they're called on. We've got together an Anglo-Saxon 'lieance in this wa-ard, an' we're goin' to ilict Sarsfield O'Brien prisidint, Hugh O'Neill Darsey vice-prisidint, Robert Immitt Clancy sicrety, an' Wolfe Tone Malone three-asurer. O'Brien'll be a good wan to have. He was in the Fenian r-raid, an' his father carrid a pike in forty-eight. An' he's in th' Clan. Besides, he has a sthrong pull with th' Ancient Ordher iv Anglo-Saxon Hibernyans.

"I tell ye, whin th' Clan an' th' Sons iv Sweden an' th' Banana Club an' th' Circle Francaize an' th' Pollacky Benivolent Society an' th' Rooshian Sons of Dinnymite an' th' Benny Brith an' th' Coffee Clutch that Schwartzmeister r-runs an' th' Tur-rnd'ye-mind an' th' Holland society an' th' Afro-Americans an' th' other

Anglo-Saxons begin f'r to raise their Anglo-Saxon battlecry, it'll be all day with th' eight or nine people in th' wurruld that has th' misfortune iv not bein' brought up Anglo-Saxons."

"They'se goin' to be a debate on th' 'lieance at th' ninety-eight picnic at Ogden's gr-rove," said Mr. Hennessy.

"P'r'aps," said Mr. Dooley, sweetly, "ye might like to borry th' loan iv an ice-pick."

On a Letter from the Front

MR. DOOLEY looked important, but affected indifference, as he mopped the bar. Mr. Hennessy, who had learned to study his friend in order to escape disagreeable complications, patiently waited for the philosopher to speak. Mr. Dooley rubbed the bar to the end, tossed the cloth into a mysterious recess with a practised movement, moved a glass or two on the shelf, cleaned his spectacles, and drew a letter from his pocket.

"Hm-m!" he said: "I have news fr'm th' fr-ront. Me nevvew, Terry Donahue, has sint me a letther tellin' me about it."

"How shud he know?" Mr. Hennessy asked.

"How shud he know, is it?" Mr. Dooley demanded warmly. "How shudden't he know? Isn't he a sojer in th' ar-rmy? Isn't it him that's down there in Sandago fightin' f'r th' honor iv th' flag, while th' likes iv you is up here livin' like a prince, an' doin' nawthin' all th' livelong day but shovel at th' rollin'-mills? Who are ye f'r to criticize th' dayfinders iv our counthry who ar-re lyin' in th' trinches, an' havin' th' clothes stole off their backs be th' pathriotic Cubians, I'd like to know? F'r two pins, Hinnissy, you an' I'd quarrel."

"I didn't mean nawthin'," Mr. Hennessy apologized. "I didn't know he was down there."

"Nayether did I," said Mr. Dooley. "But I informed mesilf. I'll have no wan in this place speak again th' ar-rmy. Ye can have ye'er say about Mack. He has a good job, an' 'tis r-right an'

36

proper f'r to baste him fr'm time to time. It shows ye'er in good thrim, an' it don't hur-rt him. They'se no wan to stop his pay. He goes up to th' cashier an' dhraws his forty-wan-sixty-six jus' th' same whether he's sick or well, an' whether he's pulled th' box reg-lar or has been playin' forty-fives in th' back room. But whin ye come to castin' aspersions on th' ar'rmy, be hivens, ye'll find that I can put me thumb on this showcase an' go over at wan lep."

"I didn't say annything," said Mr. Hennessy. "I didn't know about Terry."

"Iv coorse, ye didn't," said Mr. Dooley. "An' that's what I'm sayin'. Ye're here wallowin' in luxury, wheelin' pig ir'n fr'm morn till night; an' ye have no thought iv what's goin' on beyant. You an' Jawn D. Rockefeller an' Phil Ar-rmour an' Jay Pierpont Morgan an' th' r-rest iv ye is settin' back at home figurin' how ye can make some wan else pay ye'er taxes f'r ye. What is it to ye that me nevvew Terry is sleepin' in ditch wather an' atin' hard tacks an' coffee an' bein' r-robbed be leeber Cubians, an' catchin' yellow fever without a chanst iv givin' it to e'er a Spanyard. Ye think more iv a stamp thin ye do iv ye'er counthry. Ye're like th' Sugar Thrust. F'r two cints ye'd refuse to support th' govermint. I know ye, ye bloated monno-polist."

"I'm no such thing," said Mr. Hennessy, hotly. "I've been a Dimmycrat f'r thirty year."

"Well, annyhow," said Mr. Dooley, "don't speak disrayspictful iv th' ar-rmy. Lave me r-read you Terry's letter fr'm th' fr-ront. 'M — m: In th' trinches, two miles fr'm Sandago, with a land crab as big as a lobster crawlin' up me back be way iv Kingston, June 6, Dear Uncle Martin.' That's th' way it begins. 'Dear Uncle Martin: We are all well here, except thim that is not, an' hope ye're injyin' th' same gr-reat blessin'. It's hotter down here thin Billy-be-dam'd. They'se a rollin'-mill near here jus' th' same as at home, but all th' hands is laid off on account iv bad times. They used ol'-fashioned wooden wheelbahrs an' fired with wood. I don't think they cud handle th' pig th' way we done, bein' small la-ads. Th' coke has to be hauled up in sacks be th' gang. Th' derrick hands got six a week, but hadn't anny union. Helpers got four twenty. Puddlers was well paid. I wint through th' plant befure we come up here, an' r-run a wagon up th' plank jus' to keep me hand in. Tell me frinds that wan gang iv good la-ads fr'm th' r-road cud wurruk anny three iv th' gangs down here. Th' mills is owned be Rockefellar, so no more at prisint fr'm yer affecshunate nevvew, Peter Casey, who's writin' this f'r me.' "

" 'Tis a good letter," said Mr. Hennessy. "I don't see how they cud get derrick hands f'r six a week."

"Me frind Jawn D. knows how," said Mr. Dooley.

On Our Cuban Allies

"WELL, SIR," said Mr. Dooley, "dam thim Cubians! If I was Gin'ral Shafter, I'd back up th' wagon in front iv th' dure, an' I'd say to Gin'ral Garshy, I'd say, 'I want you'; an' I'd have thim all down at th' station an' dacently booked be th' desk sergeant befure th' fall iv night. Th' impydince iv thim!"

"What have they been doin'?" Mr. Hennessy asked.

"Failin' to undherstand our civilization," said Mr. Dooley. "Ye see, it was this way. This is th' way it was: Gin'ral Garshy with wan hundherd thousan' men's been fightin' bravely f'r two years f'r to liberyate Cubia. F'r two years he's been marchin' his sivinty-five thousan' men up an' down th' island, desthroyin' th' haughty Spanyard be th' millyons. Whin war was declared, he offered his own sarvice an' th' sarvices iv his ar-rmy iv fifty thousan' men to th' United States; an', while waitin' f'r ships to arrive, he marched at th' head iv his tin thousan' men down to Sandago de Cuba an' captured a cigar facthry, which they soon rayjooced to smokin' ruins. They was holdin' this position — Gin'ral Garshy an' his gallant wan thousan' men — whin Gin'ral Shafter arrived. Gin'ral Garshy immedjitly offered th' sarvices iv himsilf an' his two hundherd men f'r th' capture iv Sandago; an', when Gin'ral Shafter arrived, there was Gin'ral Garshy with his gallant band iv fifty Cubians, r-ready to eat at a minyit's notice.

"Gin'ral Shafter is a big, coorse, two-fisted man fr'm Mitchi-gan, an', whin he see Gin'ral Garshy an' his twinty-five gallant followers, 'Fr-ront,' says he. 'This way,' he says, 'step lively,' he says, 'an' move some iv these things,' he says. 'Sir,' says Gin'ral Garshy, 'd'ye take me f'r a dhray?' he says. 'I'm a sojer,' he says, 'not a baggage car,' he says. 'I'm a Cubian pathrite, an' I'd lay down me life an' the lives iv ivry wan iv th' eighteen brave men iv me devoted ar-rmy,' he says; 'but I'll be dam'd if I carry a thrunk,' he says. 'I'll fight whiniver 'tis cool,' he says, 'an' they ain't wan iv these twelve men here that wudden't follow me to hell if they was awake at th' time,' he says; 'but,' he says, 'if 'twas wurruk we were lookin' f'r, we cud have found it long ago,' he says. 'They'se a lot iv it in this counthry that nobody's usin',' he says. 'What we want,' he says, 'is freedom,' he says; 'an', if ye think we have been in th' woods dodgin' th' savage corryspondint f'r two year,' he says, 'f'r th' sake iv r-rushin' yer laundhry home,' he says, ''tis no wondher,' he says, 'that th' r-roads fr'm Marinette to Kalamazoo is paved with goold bricks bought be th' people iv ye'er native State,' he says.

"So Shafter had to carry his own thrunk; an' well it was f'r him that it wasn't Gin'ral Miles', the weather bein' hot. An' Shafter was mad clear through; an', whin he took hold iv Sandago, an' was sendin' out invitations, he scratched Garshy. Garshy took his gallant band iv six back to th' woods; an' there th' three iv thim ar-re now, ar-rmed with forty r-rounds iv canned lobster, an' ready to raysist to th' death. Him an' th' other man has written to Gin'ral Shafter to tell him what they think iv him, an' it don't take long."

"Well," said Mr. Hennessy, "I think Shafter done wrong. He might've asked Garshy in f'r to see th' show, seein' that he's been hangin' ar-round f'r a long time, doin' th' best he cud."

"It isn't that," explained Mr. Dooley.

"Th' throuble is th' Cubians don't undherstand our civilization. Over here freedom means hard wurruk. What is th' ambition iv all iv us, Hinnissy? 'Tis ayether to hold our job or to get wan. We want wurruk. We must have it. D'ye raymimber th' sign th' mob carrid in th' procession las' year? 'Give us wurruk, or we perish,' it said. They had their heads bate in be polismen because no philan-thropist'd come along an' make thim shovel coal. Now, in Cubia, whin th' mobs turns out, they carry a banner with the wurruds, 'Give us nawthin' to do, or we perish.'

40

Whin a Cubian comes home at night with a happy smile on his face, he don't say to his wife an' childher, 'Thank Gawd, I've got wurruk at last!' He says, 'Thank Gawd, I've been fired.' An' th' childher go out, and they say, 'Pah-pah has lost his job.' And Mrs. Cubian buys hersilf a new bonnet; and where wanst they was sorrow an' despair all is happiness an' a cottage organ.

"Ye can't make people here undherstand that, an' ye can't make a Cubian undherstand that freedom means th' same thing as a pinitinchry sintince. Whin we thry to get him to wurruk, he'll say: 'Why shud I? I haven't committed anny crime.' That's goin' to be th' throuble. Th' first thing we know we'll have another war in Cubia whin we begin disthriburtin' good jobs, twelve hours a day, wan sivinty-five. Th' Cubians ain't civilized in our way. I sometimes think I've got a touch iv Cubian blood in me own veins."

On the Destruction of
Cervera's Fleet

(These comments were made by Mr. Dooley during a strike
of the stereotypers, which caused the English newspapers
of Chicago temporarily to suspend publication.)

"I HEAR," said Mr. Hennessy, "that th' stereopticons on th'
newspapers have sthruck."

"I sh'd think they wud," said Mr. Dooley. "Th' las' time I was
down town was iliction night, whin Charter Haitch's big la-ad
was ilicted, an' they was wurrukin' th' stereopticons till they was
black in th' face. What's th' news?"

"Th' What Cheer, Ioway, Lamp iv Freedom is on th' sthreets
with a tillygram that Shafter has captured Sandago de Cuba, an'
is now settin' on Gin'ral Pando's chest with his hands in his hair.
But this is denied be th' Palo Gazoot, the Macoupin County
Raygisther, an' th' Meridyan Sthreet Afro-American. I also see
be th' Daily Scoor Card, th' Wine List, th' Deef Mute's Spokes-
man, th' Morgue Life, the Bill iv Fare, th' Stock Yards Sthraight
Steer, an' Jack's Tips on th' Races, the on'y daily paper printed
in Chicago, that Sampson's fleet is in th' Suez Canal bombarding
Cades. Th' Northwestern Christyan Advycate says this is not
thrue, but that George Dixon was outpointed be an English boxer
in a twenty-r-round go in New York."

"Ye've got things mixed up," said Mr. Dooley. "I get th' news
sthraight. 'Twas this way. Th' Spanish fleet was bottled up in
Sandago Harbor, an' they dhrew th' cork. That's a joke. I see

42

it in th' pa-apers. Th' gallant boys iv th' navy was settin' out on
th' deck, defindin' their counthry an' dhrawin' three ca-ards
apiece, whin th' Spanish admiral con-cluded 'twud be better f'r
him to be desthroyed on th' ragin' sea, him bein' a sailor, thin
to have his fleet captured be cav'lry. Annyhow, he was willin' to
take a chance; an' he says to his sailors: 'Spanyards,' he says,
'Castiles,' he says, 'we have et th' las' bed-tick,' he says; 'an', if
we stay here much longer,' he says, 'I'll have to have a steak off
th' armor plate fried f'r ye,' he says. 'Lave us go out where we
can have a r-run f'r our money,' he says. An' away they wint.
I'll say this much f'r him, he's a brave man, a dam brave man.
I don't like a Spanyard no more than ye do, Hinnissy. I niver
see wan. But, if this here man was a — was a Zulu, I'd say he
was a brave man. If I was aboord wan iv thim yachts that was
converted, I'd go to this here Cervera, an' I'd say: 'Manual,' I'd
say, 'ye're all right, me boy. Ye ought to go to a doctor an' have
ye'er eyes re-set, but ye're a good fellow. Go downstairs,' I'd say,
'an' open th' cupboard jus' nex' to th' head iv th' bed, an' find
th' bottle marked "Floridy Wather," an' threat ye'er-silf kindly.'
That's what I'd say to Cervera. He's all right.

"Well, whin our boys see th' Spanish fleet comin' out iv th'
harbor, they gathered on th' deck an' sang th' naytional anthem,
'They'll be a hot time in th' ol' town tonight.' A lift-nant come
up to where Admiral Sampson was settin' playin' sivin up with
Admiral Schley. 'Bill,' he says, 'th' Spanish fleet is comin' out,'
he says. 'What talk have ye?' says Sampson. 'Sind out some row-
boats an' a yacht, an' desthroy thim. Clubs is thrumps,' he says,
and he wint on playin'. Th' Spanish fleet was attackted on all
sides be our br-rave la-ads, nobly assisted be th' dispatch boats
iv the newspapers. Wan by wan they was desthroyed. Three
battleships attackted th' converted yacht Gloucester. Th'
Gloucester used to be owned be Pierpont Morgan; but 'twas
converted, an' is now leadin' a dacint life. Th' Gloucester sunk
thim all, th' Christobell Comma, the Viscera, an' th' Admiral
O'Quinn. It thin wint up to two Spanish torpedo boats an' giv
thim wan punch, an' away they wint. Be this time th' sojers had
heerd of the victhry, an' they gathered on th' shore, singin' th'
naytional anthem, 'They'll be a hot time in th' ol' town to-night,
me babby.' Th' gloryous ol' chune, to which Washington an'

43

Grant an' Lincoln marched, was took up be th' sailors on th' ships, an' Admiral Cervera r-run wan iv his boats ashore, an' jumped into th' sea. At last accounts th' followin' dispatches had been received: 'To Willum McKinley: Congratulations on ye'er noble victhry. (Signed) Willum McKinley.' 'To Russell A. Alger: Ye done splendid. (Signed) Russell A. Alger.' 'To James Wilson, Sicrety iv Agriculture: This is a gr-reat day f'r Ioway. Ar-re ye much hur-rted? (Signed) James Wilson.' '

"Where did ye hear all this?" asked Mr. Hennessy, in great amazement.

"I r-read it," said Mr. Dooley, impressively, "in the Staats Zeitung."

On a Letter to Mr. Depew

"I USEN'T to know," said Mr. Dooley, "what me frind Gin'ral Sherman meant whin he said that thing about war. I've been through two iv thim, not to speak iv convintions an' prim'ries, an' divvle th' bit iv har-rm come to me no more thin if I was settin' on a roof playin' an accorjeen. But I know now what th' ol' la-ad meant. He meant war was hell whin 'twas over.

"I ain't heerd anny noice fr'm th' fellows that wint into threnches an' plugged th' villyanious Spanyard. Most iv thim is too weak to kick. But th' proud an' fearless pathrites who restrained thimsilves, an' didn't go to th' fr-ront, th' la-ads that sthruggled hard with their warlike tindincies, an' fin'lly downed thim an' stayed at home an' practised up upon th' typewriter, they're ragin' an' tearin' an' desthroyin' their foes.

"Did ye see what me frind Alger wrote to Chansy Depoo? Well, sir, Alger has been misthreated. There's a good man. I say he's a good man. An' he is, too. At anny thrick fr'm shingles to two-be-fours he's as good as th' best. But no wan apprechated Alger. No wan undherstud him. No wan even thried to. Day be day he published th' private letters iv other people, an' that didn't throw anny light on his charackter. Day be day he had his pitchers took, an' still th' people didn't get onto th' cur-rves iv him. Day be day he chatted iv th' turrors iv war, an' still people on'y said: 'An' Alger also r-ran.' But th' time come whin

Alger cud contain himsilf no longer, an' he set down an' wrote to Chansy Depoo.

" 'Mr. Chansy Depot, care iv Grand Cintral Depew, New York, N.Y., Esquire. Dear Chanse: I've been expectin' a letter fr'm ye f'r three or four days. In reply to same will say: Oh, Chanse, ye don't know how I suffer. I'm that low in me mind I feel like a bunch iv lathes. Oh, dear, to think iv what I've gone through. I wint into th' war onprepared. I had on'y so many r-rounds iv catridges an' a cross-cut saw, an' I failed to provide mesilf with th' ord'nary necessities iv life. But, in spite iv me deficiencies, I wint bravely ahead. Th' sthrain was something tur-r'ble on me. Me mind give out repeatedly. I cud not think at times, but I niver faltered. In two months I had enough supplies piled up in Maine to feed ivry sojer in Cubia. They were thousands iv r-rounds iv catridges f'r ivry rig'mint, and all th' rig'mints had to do was to write f'r thim. Th' navy had taken Manila an' Cervera's fleet, an' th' ar-rmy had taken Sandago an' th' yellow fever. Th' war is over, an' peace wanst more wags her wings over th' counthry. Pine scantlings is quoted sthrong. Ivrywhere is peace an' con-tint. Me photographs are on sale at all first-class newsdealers. Yet there is no ca'm f'r me. Onthinkin' wans insult me. They tell me a sojer can't ate gin'ral ordhers. They want me to raysign an' go back to me humble home in Mitchigan. Disgustin' men that've done nawthin' but get thimsilves shot, ask f'r milk an' quinine. They'll be askin' me to carry food to thim nex'. Oh, Chanse, oh, hivens, ye can't know how grieved I am! Rather wud I have perished in a log jam thin to've indured this ingratichood. But, in lookin' back over me past life, I can think iv no wrong I've done. If me mim'ry is at fault, please note. Me career is an open book. I've held nawthin' back fr'm th' public, not even whin 'twas mar-rked private. I can say with th' pote that I done me jooty. But, oh, Chanse! don't iver aspire to my job. Be sicrety of war, if ye will; but niver be sicrety iv A war. Do not offer this letter to th' newspapers. Make thim take it. How's things goin' with ye, ol' pal? I hope to see ye at th' seaside. Till thin, I'm yours, sick at heart, but atin' reg'lar. RUSS.' "

"Well," said Mr. Hennessy, "th' poor man must've had a har-rd time iv it."

"He did," said Mr. Dooley. "Niver laid his head to a pillow befure eight, up with th' moon: he 's suffered as no man can tell. But he'll be all r-right whin his mind's at r-rest."

On the President's Cat

" 'Twas this way about Dr. Huckenlooper. Mack has a cat that was give him f'r a Chris'mas prisint be me frind Pierpont Morgan, an' th' cat was a gr-reat favor-ite in th' White House. 'Twas as quite as th' Sicrety iv Agriculture an' as affectionate as th' Sicrety iv th' Three-asury. Th' cat was called Goold Bonds, because iv th' inthrest he dhrew. He very often played with th' Sicrety iv th' Navy, an' ivry wan that come to th' White House f'r a job loved him.

"But wan day Goold Bonds begun to look bad. He cudden't ate th' r-rich crame out iv th' di'mon'-studded saucer. He stopped castin' an eye at th' c'nary in th' cage. Whin th' Sicrety iv th' Navy wint down f'r to play with him, Goold Bonds spit at that good an' gr-reat man. Mack was shavin' himsilf befure th' lookin'-glass, an' had jus' got his face pulled r-round to wan side f'r a good gash, whin he heerd a scream iv ag'ny behind him, an' tur-rned to see Goold Bonds leap up with his paws on his stomach an' hit th' ceilin'. Mack give a cry iv turror, an' grabbed at Goold Bonds. Away wint Goold Bonds through th' house. Th' Sicrety iv War seen him comin', an' called, 'Pussy, pussy.' Goold Bonds wint through his legs, an' galloped f'r where th' Postmaster-gin'ral was settin' editin' his pa-aper. Th' Postmaster-gin'ral had jus' got as far as 'we opine,' whin he see Goold Bonds, an' he bate th' cat to th' windy be a whisker.

48

"Well, Goold Bonds ended up in th' coal cellar, an' they was a cab'net council f'r to see what was to be done. 'Sind f'r Doctor Heinegagubler,' says th' Sicrety iv War. 'He's wan iv th' gr-reatest surgeons iv our time,' he says, 'an' can cure annything fr'm pips to glanders,' he says. Th' famous Doctor Honeycooler was summoned. 'Sir,' says Mack, 'Goold Bonds, th' pride iv th' administhration, has had a fit,' he says. ' 'Twud br-reak our hear-rts to lose our little pet,' he says. 'Go,' he says, 'an' take such measures as ye'er noble healin' ar-rt sug-gists,' he says; 'an' may th' prayers iv an agonized foster-parent go with ye,' he says. An' Doctor Higgenlocker wint down into th' coal-shed; an' whin he come back, it was with Goold Bonds in his ar-rms, weak an' pale, but with a wan smile on his lips.

"Afther embracin' Goold Bonds an' tuckin' him away in bed, Mack tur-rns to th' Dock. 'Dock,' he says, 'ye have performed a noble sarvice,' he says. 'I appint ye a major-gin'ral,' he says. 'I'm that already,' says th' Dock. 'I've r-rich relatives in Philadelphia,' he says. 'But,' says Mack, ' 'tis a shame to think iv ye'er noble sarvices bein' wasted,' he says, 'whin ye'er counthry calls,' he says. 'I appint ye,' he says, 'surgeon-gin'ral,' he says. 'Proceed,' he says, 'to Cubia, an' stamp out th' dhread ravages,' he says, 'iv r-ringbone an' staggers,' he says.

"That's how Dock got th' job. He was a gr-reat man down there, an' now he's wan iv th' vethranaryans iv th' war. Ye heerd iv typhoid an' yellow fever in th' threnches; but did ye hear annything iv spavin or th' foot-an'-mouth disease? Not wanst. Dock was on jooty late an' early. Sleepless an' vigilant, he stood beside th' suffrin' mules, allayin' their pain, an' slowly but surely dhraggin' thim out iv th' clutches iv pink-eye an' epizootic. He had a cheery wurrud, a pleasant smile, an' a bottle iv liniment f'r wan an' all. He cured Teddy Rosenfelt's hor-rse iv intherference an' made a soothin' lotion iv axle-grease f'r Gin'ral Shafter's buckboard. Ye might see him anny time wandhrin' through th' camp with a hatful of oats or a wisp of hay. They called him th' Stall Angel, and countless thousands iv sick hor-rses blessed him. He's a gr-reat man is th' Dock. But, if it hadn't been f'r Goold Bonds, th' counthry wud niver have had his sarvices. Who knows but that Mack's cat was th' rale victhor at Sandago?"

"Didn't he cure anny men?" asked Mr. Hennessy.

"Sure," said Mr. Dooley. "He cured Teddy Rosenfelt iv boltin'."

On a Speech by President McKinley

"I HEAR-R that Mack's in town," said Mr. Dooley.

"Didn't ye see him?" asked Mr. Hennessy.

"Faith, I did not!" said Mr. Dooley. "If 'tis meetin' me he's afther, all he has to do is to get on a ca-ar an' r-ride out to number nine-double-naught-nine Archey R-road, an' stop whin he sees th' sign iv th' Tipp'rary Boodweiser Brewin' Company. I'm here fr'm eight in the mornin' till midnight, an' th' r-rest iv th' time I'm in the back room in th' ar-rms iv Or-rphyus, as Hogan says. Th' Presidint is as welcome as anny rayspictable marrid man. I will give him a chat an' a dhrink f'r fifteen cints; an', as we're not, as a frind iv mine in th' grocery an' pothry business says, intirely a commercial an' industhreel nation, if he has th' Sicrety iv th' Threasury with him, I'll give thim two f'r twenty-five cints, which is th' standard iv value among civilized nations th' wurruld over. Prisidint iv th' United States, says ye? Well, I'm prisidint iv this liquor store, fr'm th' pitcher iv th' Chicago fire above th' wash-stand in th' back room to th' dure-step. Beyond that belongs to th' polisman on th' bate. An Amur-rican's home, as wan iv th' potes says, is his castle till th' morgedge falls due. An' divvle a fut will I put out iv this dure to see e'er a prisidint, prince, or potentate, fr'm th' czar iv Rooshia to th' king iv Chiny. There's Prisidint Mack at th' Audjiotoroom, an' here's Prisidint Dooley at nine-double-naught-nine, an' th' len'th iv th' sthreet between thim. Says he, 'Come over to th' hotel

51

an' see me.' Says I, 'If ye find ye'ersilf thrun fr'm a ca-ar in me neighborhood, dhrop in.' An' there ye ar-re.

"I may niver see him. I may go to me grave without gettin' an' eye on th' wan man besides mesilf that don't know what th' furrin' policy iv th' United States is goin' to be. An he, poor man, whin some wan asts him, 'Did ye iver meet Dooley?' 'll have to say, 'No, I had th' chanst wanst, but me accursed pride kept me from visitin' him.'

"I r-read his speeches, though, an' know what he's doin'. Some iv thim ar-re gr-reat. He attinded th' banket given be th' Prospurity Brigade at th' hotel where he's stoppin'. 'Twas a magnificent assimblage iv th' laborin' classes, costin' fifteen dollars a plate, an' on'y disturbed whin a well-to-do gintleman in th' dhry-goods business had to be thrun out f'r takin' a kick at a waiter. I r-read be th' papers that whin Mack come in he was rayceived be th' gatherin' with shouts iv approval. Th' proceedin's was opened with a prayer that Providence might r-remain undher th' protection iv th' administhration. Th' Sicrety iv th' Treasury followed with a gran' speech, highly commindin' th' action iv th' threasury department durin' th' late war; 'but,' says he, 'I cannot,' he says, 'so far forget mesilf,' he says, 'as not to mintion,' he says, 'that,' he says, 'if it hadn't been f'r the sublime pathreetism an' courage,' he says, 'iv th' gintleman whom we honor,' he says, 'in puttin' me on th' foorce,' he says, 'I might not be here tonight,' he says.

"Th' Sicrety iv th' Threasury was followed be th' Gin'ral Shafter. 'Gintlemen,' says he, 'it gives me,' he says, 'gr-reat pleasure,' he says, 'to be prisint in th' mist iv so manny an' so various vittles,' he says. 'Iv coorse,' he says, 'I re-elize me own gr-reat worth,' he says; 'but,' he says, 'I wud have to be more thin human,' he says, 'to overlook th' debt iv gratichood,' he says, 'th' counthry owes,' he says, 'to th' man whose foresight, wisdom, an' prudence brought me for-ard at such an opparchune time,' he says. 'Gintlemen,' he says, 'onless ye have lived in th' buckboard f'r months on th' parched deserts iv Cubia,' he says, 'ye little know what a pleasure it is,' he says, 'to dhrink,' he says, 'to th' author iv our bein' here,' he says. An' Gin-ral Miles wint out an' punched th' bell-boy. Mack r-rose up in a perfect hurcane iv applause, an' says he, 'Gintlemen,' he says, 'an' fellow-heroes,' he says, 'ye do me too much honor,' he says. 'I alone shud not have th' credit iv this gloryous victhry. They ar-re others.' (A voice: 'Shafter.' Another voice: 'Gage.' Another voice: 'Dooley.') 'But I pass to a more conganial line iv thought,' he says. 'We have just emerged fr'm a turrible war,' he says. 'Again,' he says, 'we ar-re a united union,' he says. 'No north,' he says, 'no south, no east,' he says, 'no west. No north east a point east,' he says. 'Th' inimies iv our counthry has been cr-rushed,' he says, 'or is stuck down in Floridy with his rig'mint talkin',' he says, 'his hellish docthrines to th' allygatars,' he says. 'Th' nation is wanst more at peace undher th' gran' goold standard,' he says. 'Now,' he says, 'th' question is what shall we do with th' fruits iv victhry?' he says. (A voice, 'Can thim.') 'Our duty to civilization commands us to be up an' doin',' he says. 'We ar-re bound,' he says, 'to—to re-elize our destiny, whativer it may be,' he says. 'We can not tur-rn back,' he says, 'th' hands iv th' clock that, even as I speak,' he says, 'is r-rushin' through th' hear-rts iv men,' he says, 'dashin' its spray against th' star iv liberty an' hope, an' no north, no south, no east, no west, but a steady purpose to do th' best we can, considerin' all th' circumstances iv the case,' he says. 'I hope I have made th' matther clear to ye,' he says, 'an', with these few remarks,' he says, 'I will tur-rn th' job over to destiny,' he says, 'which is sure to lead us iver on an' on, an' back an' forth, a united an' happy people, livin',' he says, 'undher an adminis-thration that, thanks to our worthy Prisidint an' his cap-ble an' earnest advisers, is second to none,' he says."

"What do you think ought to be done with th' fruits iv victhry?" Mr. Hennessy asked.

"Well," said Mr. Dooley, "if 'twas up to me, I'd eat what was r-ripe an' give what wasn't r-ripe to me inimy. An' I guess that's what Mack means."

On the Hero in Politics

" 'TIS as much as a man's life is worth these days," said Mr. Dooley, "to have a vote. Look here," he continued, diving under the bar and producing a roll of paper. "Here's th' pitchers iv candydates I pulled down fr'm th' windy, an' jus' knowin' they're here makes me that nervous f'r th' contints iv th' cash dhrawer I'm afraid to tur-rn me back f'r a minyit. I'm goin' to throw thim out in th' back yard.

"All heroes, too, Hinnissy. They'se Mike O'Toole, th' hero iv Sandago, that near lost his life be dhrink on his way to th' arm'ry, an' had to be sint home without lavin' th' city. There's Turror Teddy Mangan, th' night man at Flaher-ty's, that loaded th' men that loaded th' guns that kilt th' mules at Matoonzas. There's Hero O'Brien, that wud've inlisted if he hadn't been too old, an' th' contractin' business in such good shape. There's Bill Cory, that come near losin' his life at a cinematograph iv th' battle iv Manila. They're all here, bedad, r-ready to sarve their country to th' bitter end, an' to r-rush, voucher in hand, to th' city threasurer's office at a minyit's notice.

"I wint to a hero meetin' th' other night, Hinnissy, an' that's sthrange f'r me. Whin a man gets to be my age, he laves th' shoutin' f'r th' youth iv th' land, onless he has a pol-itical job. I niver had a job but wanst. That was whin I was precin't cap'n; an' a good wan I was, too. None bether. I'd been on th' cinthral co-mity to-day, but f'r me losin' ambition whin they r-run a man

54

be th' name iv Eckstein f'r aldherman. I was sayin', Hinnissy, whin a man gets to be my age, he ducks pol-itical meetin's, an' r-reads th' papers an' weighs th' ividence an' th' argymints,— pro-argymints an' con-argy-mints,—an' makes up his mind ca'mly, an' votes th' Dimmycratic ticket. But young Dorsey he med me go with him to th' hero's meetin' in Finucane's hall.

"Well, sir, there was O'Toole an' all th' rest on th' platform in unyform, with flags over thim, an' the bands playin' 'They'll be a hot time in th' ol' town to-night again'; an' th' chairman was Plunkett. Ye know Plunkett: a good man if they was no gr-rand juries. He was makin' a speech. 'Whin th' battle r-raged,' he says, 'an' th' bullets fr'm th' haughty Spanyards' raypeatin' Mouser r-rifles,' he says, 'where was Cassidy?' he says. 'In his saloon,' says I, 'in I'mrald Av'noo,' says I. 'Thrue f'r ye,' says Plunkett. 'An' where,' he says, 'was our candydate?' he says. 'In somebody else's saloon,' says I. 'No,' says he. 'Whin th' Prisidint,' he says, 'called th' nation to ar-rms,' he says, 'an' Congress voted fifty million good bucks f'r th' nayional definse,' he says, 'Thomas Francis Dorgan,' he says, 'in that minyit iv nayional pearl,' says he, 'left his good job in the pipe-yard,' he says, 'an' wint down to th' raycruitin' office, an' says, "How manny calls f'r volunteers is out?" he says. "Wan," says th' officer. "Put me down," says Dorgan, "f'r th' tenth call," he says. This, gintlemen iv th' foorth precin't,' he says, 'is Thomas Francis Dorgan, a man who, if ilicted,' he says, 'victhry'll perch,' he says, 'upon our banners,' he says; 'an',' he says, 'th' nayional honor will be maintained,' he says, 'in th' county boord,' he says.

"I wint out to take th' air, an' I met me frind Clohessy, th' little tailor fr'm Halsted Sthreet. Him an' me had a shell iv beer together at th' German's; an' says I, 'What d'ye think iv th' heroes?' I says. 'Well,' says he, 'I make no doubt 'twas brave iv Dorgan,' he says, 'f'r to put his name in f'r th' tenth call,' he says; 'but,' he says, 'I don't like Plunkett, an' it seems to me a man'd have to be a hell iv a sthrong man, even if he was a hero, to be Plunkett's man, an' keep his hands out iv ye'er pockets,' he says. 'I'm with Clancy's candydate,' he says. 'He niver offered to enlist for th' war,' he says, 'but 'twas Clancy put Terence on th' polis foorce an' got th' school f'r Aggie,' he says.

"That's the way I feel," said Mr. Hennessy. "I wudden't thrust

Plunkett as far as I cud throw a cow be th' tail. If Dorgan was Clancy's war hero, I'd be with him."

"Annyhow," said Mr. Dooley, "mighty few iv th' rale heroes iv th' war is r-runnin' f'r office. Most iv thim put on their blue overalls whin they was mustered out an' wint up an' ast f'r their ol' jobs back—an' sometimes got thim. Ye can see as manny as tin iv thim at the rollin'-mills defindin' th' nation's honor with wheelbahr's an' a slag shovel."

MR. DOOLEY IN PEACE

On New Year's Resolutions

MR. HENNESSY looked out at the rain dripping down in Archey Road, and sighed, "A-ha, 'tis a bad spell iv weather we're havin'."

"Faith, it is," said Mr. Dooley, "or else we mind it more thin we did. I can't remimber wan day fr'm another. Whin I was young, I niver thought iv rain or snow, cold or heat. But now th' heat stings an' th' cold wrenches me bones; an', if I go out in th' rain with less on me thin a ton iv rubber, I'll pay dear f'r it in achin' j'ints, so I will. That's what old age means; an' now another year has been put on to what we had befure, an' we're expected to be gay. 'Ring out th' old,' says a guy at th' Brothers' School. 'Ring out th' old, ring in th' new,' he says. 'Ring out th' false, ring in th' thrue,' says he. It's a pretty sintimint, Hinnissy; but how ar-re we goin' to do it? Nawthin'd please me betther thin to turn me back on th' wicked an' ingloryous past, rayform me life, an' live at peace with th' wurruld to th' end iv me days. But how th' divvle can I do it? As th' fellow says, 'Can th' leopard change his spots,' or can't he?

"You know Dorsey, iv coorse, th' cross-eyed May-o man that come to this counthry about wan day in advance iv a warrant f'r sheep-stealin'? Ye know what he done to me, tellin' people I was caught in me cellar poorin' wather into a bar'l? Well, last night says I to mesilf, thinkin' iv Dorsey, I says: 'I swear that henceforth I'll keep me temper with me fellow-men. I'll not let anger or jealousy get th' betther iv me,' I says. 'I'll lave off all

59

me old feuds; an' if I meet me inimy goin' down th' sthreet, I'll go up an' shake him be th' hand, if I'm sure he hasn't a brick in th' other hand.' Oh, I was mighty compliminthry to mesilf. I set be th' stove dhrinkin' hot wans, an' ivry wan I dhrunk made me more iv a pote. 'Tis th' way with th' stuff. Whin I'm in dhrink, I have manny a fine thought; an', if I wasn't too comfortable to go an' look f'r th' ink-bottle, I cud write pomes that'd make Shakespeare an' Mike Scanlan think they were wur-rkin' on a dredge. 'Why,' says I, 'carry into th' new year th' hathreds iv th' old?' I says. 'Let th' dead past bury its dead,' says I. 'Tur-rn ye'er lamps up to th' blue sky,' I says. (It was rainin' like th' divvle, an' th' hour was midnight; but I give no heed to that, bein' comfortable with th' hot wans.) An' I wint to th' dure, an', whin Mike Duffy come by on number wan hundherd an' five, ringin' th' gong iv th' ca-ar, I hollered to him: 'Ring out th' old, ring in th' new.' 'Go back into ye'er stall,' he says, 'an' wring ye'ersilf out,' he says. 'Ye'er wet through,' he says.

"Whin I woke up this mornin', th' pothry had all disappeared, an' I begun to think th' las' hot wan I took had somethin' wrong with it. Besides, th' lumbago was grippin' me till I cud hardly put wan foot befure th' other. But I remimbered me promises to mesilf, an' I wint out on th' sthreet, intindin' to wish ivry wan a 'Happy New Year,' an' hopin' in me hear-rt that th' first wan I wished it to'd tell me to go to th' divvle, so I cud hit him in th' eye. I hadn't gone half a block befure I spied Dorsey acrost th' sthreet. I picked up a half a brick an' put it in me pocket, an' Dorsey done th' same. Thin we wint up to each other. 'A Happy New Year,' says I. 'Th' same to you,' says he, 'an' manny iv thim,' he says. 'Ye have a brick in ye'er hand,' says I. 'I was thinkin' iv givin' ye a New Year's gift,' says he. 'Th' same to you, an' manny iv thim,' says I, fondlin' me own ammunition. "'Tis even all around,' says he. 'It is,' says I. 'I was thinkin' las' night I'd give up me gredge again ye,' says he. 'I had th' same thought mesilf,' says I. 'But, since I seen ye'er face,' he says, 'I've con-cluded that I'd be more comfortable hatin' ye thin havin' ye f'r a frind,' says he. 'Ye're a man iv taste,' says I. An' we backed away fr'm each other. He's a Tip, an' can throw a stone like a rifleman; an', Hinnissy, I'm somethin' iv an amachoor shot with a half-brick mesilf.

"Well, I've been thinkin' it over, an' I've argied it out that life'd not be worth livin' if we didn't keep our inimies. I can have all th' frinds I need. Anny man can that keeps a liquor sthore. But a rale sthrong inimy, specially a May-o inimy,—wan that hates ye ha-ard, an' that ye'd take th' coat off yer back to do a bad tur-rn to,—is a luxury that I can't go without in me ol' days. Dorsey is th' right sort. I can't go by his house without bein' in fear he'll spill th' chimbly down on me head; an', whin he passes my place, he walks in th' middle iv th' sthreet, an' crosses himsilf. I'll swear off on annything but Dorsey. He's a good man, an' I despise him. Here's long life to him."

On Gold-seeking

"WELL, sir," said Mr. Hennessy, "that Alaska's th' gr-reat place. I thought 'twas nawthin' but an iceberg with a few seals roostin' on it, an' wan or two hundherd Ohio politicians that can't be killed on account iv th' threaty iv Pawrs. But here they tell me 'tis fairly smothered in goold. A man stubs his toe on th' ground, an lifts th' top off iv a goold mine. Ye go to bed at night, an' wake up with goold fillin' in ye'er teeth."

"Yes," said Mr. Dooley, "Clancy's son was in here this mornin', an' he says a frind iv his wint to sleep out in th' open wan night, an' whin he got up his pants assayed four ounces iv goold to th' pound, an' his whiskers panned out as much as thirty dollars net."

"If I was a young man an' not tied down here," said Mr. Hennessy, "I'd go there: I wud so."

"I wud not," said Mr. Dooley. "Whin I was a young man in th' ol' counthry, we heerd th' same story about all America. We used to set be th' tur-rf fire o' nights, kickin' our bare legs on th' flure an' wishin' we was in New York, where all ye had to do was to hold ye'er hat an' th' goold guineas'd dhrop into it. An' whin I got to be a man, I come over here with a ham and a bag iv oatmeal, as sure that I'd return in a year with money enough to dhrive me own ca-ar as I was that me name was Martin Dooley. An' that was a cinch.

"But, faith, whin I'd been here a week, I seen that there was nawthin' but mud undher th' pavement,—I larned that be means iv a pick-axe at tin shillin's th' day,—an' that, though there was plenty iv goold, thim that had it were froze to it; an' I come west, still lookin' f'r mines. Th' on'y mine I sthruck at Pittsburgh was a hole f'r sewer pipe. I made it. Siven shillin's th' day. Smaller thin New York, but th' livin' was cheaper, with Mon'gahela rye at five a throw, put ye'er hand around th' glass.

"I was still dreamin' goold, an' I wint down to Saint Looey. Th' nearest I come to a fortune there was findin' a quarther on th' sthreet as I leaned over th' dashboord iv a car to whack th' off mule. Whin I got to Chicago, I looked around f'r the goold mine. They was Injuns here thin. But they wasn't anny mines I cud see. They was mud to be shovelled an' dhrays to be dhruv an' beats to be walked. I choose th' dhray; f'r I was niver cut out f'r a copper, an' I'd had me fill iv excavatin'. An' I dhruv th' dhray till I wint into business.

'Me experyence with goold minin' is it's always in th' nex' county. If I was to go to Alaska, they'd tell me iv th' finds in Seeberya. So I think I'll stay here. I'm a silver man, annyhow; an' I'm contint if I can see goold wanst a year, whin some prominent citizen smiles over his newspaper. I'm thinkin' that ivry man has a goold mine undher his own dure-step or in his neighbor's pocket at th' farthest.'

"Well, annyhow," said Mr. Hennessy, "I'd like to kick up th' sod, an' find a ton iv goold undher me fut."

"What wud ye do if ye found it?" demanded Mr. Dooley.

"I—I dinnaw," said Mr. Hennessy, whose dreaming had not gone this far. Then, recovering himself, he exclaimed with great enthusiasm, "I'd throw up me job an'—an' live like a prince."

"I tell ye what ye'd do," said Mr. Dooley. "Ye'd come back here an' sthrut up an' down th' sthreet with ye'er thumbs in ye'er armpits; an' ye'd dhrink too much, an' ride in sthreet ca-ars. Thin ye'd buy foldin' beds an' piannies, an' start a reel estate office. Ye'd be fooled a good deal an' lose a lot iv ye'er money, an' thin ye'd tighten up. Ye'd be in a cold fear night an' day that ye'd lose ye'er fortune. Ye'd wake up in th' middle iv th' night, dhreamin' that ye was back at th' gas-house with ye'er money gone. Ye'd be prisidint iv a charitable society. Ye'd have to wear ye'er shoes in th' house, an' ye'er wife'd have ye around to rayciptions an dances.' Ye'd move to Mitchigan Avnoo, an' ye'd hire a coachman that'd laugh at ye. Ye'er boys'd be joods an' ashamed iv ye, an' ye'd support ye'er daughters' husbands. Ye'd rackrint ye'er tinants an' lie about ye'er taxes. Ye'd go back to Ireland on a visit, an' put on airs with ye'er cousin Mike. Ye'd be a mane, close-fisted, onscrupulous ol' curmudgeon; an', whin ye'd die, it'd take half ye'er fortune f'r rayqueems to put ye r-right. I don't want ye iver to speak to me whin ye get rich, Hinnissy."

"I won't," said Mr. Hennessey.

On Books

"IVRY time I pick up me mornin' paper to see how th' scrap come out at Batthry D," said Mr. Dooley,", "th' first thing I r-run acrost is somethin' like this: 'A hot an' handsome gift f'r Christmas is Lucy Ann Patzooni's "Jims iv Englewood Thought" '; or 'If ye wud delight th' hear-rt iv yer child, ye'll give him Dr. Harper's monymental histhry iv th' Jewish thribes fr'm Moses to Dhryfuss' or 'Ivrybody is r-readin' Roodyard Kiplin's "Busy Pomes f'r Busy People." ' Th' idee iv givin' books f'r Christmas prisints whin th' stores are full iv tin hor-rns an' dhrums an' boxin' gloves an choo-choo ca-ars! People must be crazy."

"They ar-re," said Mr. Hennessy. "My house is so full iv books ye cudden't tur-rn around without stumblin' over thim. I found th' life iv an ex-convict, the 'Prisoner iv Zinders,' in me high hat th' other day, where Mary Ann was hidin' it fr'm her sister. Instead iv th' childher fightin' an' skylarkin' in th' evenin', they're settin' around th' table with their noses glued into books. Th' ol' woman doesn't read, but she picks up what's goin' on. 'Tis 'Honoria, did Lor-rd What's-his-name marry th' fair Aminta?' or 'But that Lady Jane was a case.' An' so it goes. There's no injymint in th' house, an' they're usin' me cravats f'r bookmarks."

" 'Tis all wrong," said Mr. Dooley. "They're on'y three books in th' wurruld worth readin',—Shakespeare, th' Bible, an' Mike Ahearn's histhry iv Chicago. I have Shakespeare on thrust, Father Kelly r-reads th' Bible f'r me, an' I didn't buy Mike Ahearn's histhry because I seen more thin he cud put into it. Books is th' roon iv people, specially novels. Whin I was a young man, th' parish priest used to preach again thim; but nobody knowed what he meant. At that time Willum Joyce had th' on'y library in th' Sixth Wa-ard. Th' mayor give him th' bound volumes iv th' council proceedings, an' they was a very handsome set. Th' on'y books I seen was th' kind that has th' life iv th' pope on th' outside an' a set iv dominos on th' inside. They're good readin'. Nawthin' cud be better f'r a man whin he's tired out afther a day's wurruk thin to go to his library an' take down wan iv th' gr-reat wurruks iv lithratchoor an' play a game iv dominos f'r th' dhrinks out iv it. Anny other kind iv r-readin', barrin' th' newspapers, which will niver hurt anny onedycated man, is desthructive iv morals.

"I had it out with Father Kelly th' other day in this very matther. He was comin' up fr'm down town with an ar-rmful iv books f'r prizes at th' school. 'Have ye th' Key to Heaven there?' says I. 'No,' says he, 'th' childher that'll get these books don't need no key. They go in under th' turnstile,' he says, laughin'. 'Have ye th' Lives iv th' Saints, or the Christyan Dooty, or th' Story iv Saint Rose iv Lima?' I says. 'I have not,' says he. 'I have some good story books. I'd rather th' kids'd r-read Charles Dickens than anny iv th' tales iv thim holy men that was burned in ile or et up be lines,' he says. 'It does no good in these degin'rate days to prove that th' best that can come to a man f'r behavin' himsilf is to be cooked in a pot or di-gisted be a line,' he says. 'Ye're wrong,' says I. 'Beggin' ye'er riv'rince's pardon, ye're wrong,' I says. 'What ar-re ye goin' to do with thim young wans? Ye're goin' to make thim near-sighted an' round-shouldered,' I says. 'Ye're goin' to have thim believe that, if they behave thim-silves an' lead a virchous life, they'll marry rich an' go to Congress. They'll wake up some day, an' find out that gettin' money an behavin' ye'ersilf don't always go together,' I says. 'Some iv th' wickedest men in th' wur-ruld have marrid rich,' I says. 'Ye're goin' to teach thim that a man doesn't have to use an ax to get along in th' wur-ruld. Ye're goin' to teach thim that a la-ad with a curlin' black mustache an' smokin' a cigareet is always a villyan, whin he's more often a barber with a lar-rge family. Life, says ye! There's no life in a book. If ye want to show thim what life is, tell thim to look around thim. There's more life on a Saturdah night in th' Ar-rchy Road thin in all th' books fr'm Shakespeare to th' rayport iv th' drainage thrustees. No man,' I says, 'iver wrote a book if he had annything to write about, except Shakespeare an' Mike Ahearn. Shakespeare was all r-right. I niver read anny of his pieces, but they sound good; an' I know Mike Ahearn is all r-right.' "

"What did he say?" asked Mr. Hennessy.

"He took it all r-right," said Mr. Dooley. "He kind o' grinned, an' says he: 'What ye say is thrue, an' it's not thrue,' he says. 'Books is f'r thim that can't injye thimsilves in anny other way,' he says. 'If ye're in good health, an' ar-re atin' three squares a day, an' not ayether sad or very much in love with ye'er lot, but just lookin' on an' not carin' a' — he said rush — 'not carin' a rush, ye don't need books,' he says. 'But if ye're a down-spirited thing an' want to get away an' can't, ye need books. 'Tis bether to be comfortable at home thin to go to th' circus, an' 'tis bether to go to th' circus thin to r-read anny book. But 'tis bether to r-read a book thin to want to go to th' circus an' not be able to,' he says. 'Well,' says I, 'whin I was growin' up, half th' con-gregation heard mass with their prayer books tur-rned upside down, an' they were as pious as anny. Th' Apostles' Creed niver was as con-vincin' to me afther I larned to r-read it as it was whin I cudden't read it, but believed it.' "

On Reform Candidates

"THAT frind iv ye'ers, Dugan, is an intilligent man," said Mr. Dooley. "All he needs is an index an' a few illusthrations to make him a bicyclopedja iv useless information."

"Well," said Mr. Hennessy, judiciously, "he ain't no Soc-rates an' he ain't no answers-to-questions colum; but he's a good man that goes to his jooty, an' as handy with a pick as some people are with a cocktail spoon. What's he been doin' again ye?"

"Nawthin'," said Mr. Dooley, "but he was in here Choosday. 'Did ye vote?' says I. 'I did,' says he. 'Which wan iv th' distinguished bunko steerers got ye'er invalu'ble suffrage?' says I. 'I didn't have none with me,' says he, 'but I voted f'r Charter Haitch,' says he. 'I've been with him in six ilictions,' says he, 'an' he's a good man,' he says. 'D'ye think ye're votin' f'r th' best?' says I. 'Why, man alive,' I says, 'Charter Haitch was assassinated three years ago,' I says. 'Was he?' says Dugan. 'Ah, well, he's lived that down be this time. He was a good man,' he says.

"Ye see, that's what thim rayform lads wint up again. If I liked rayformers, Hinnissy, an' wanted f'r to see thim win out wanst in their lifetime, I'd buy thim each a suit iv chilled steel, ar-rm thim with raypeatin' rifles, an' take thim east iv State Sthreet an' south iv Jackson Bullyvard. At prisint th' opinion that prevails in th' ranks iv th' gloryous ar-rmy iv ray-form is that there ain't annything worth seein' in this lar-rge an' commodyous desert but th' pest-house an' the bridewell. Me frind Willum J.

68

O'Brien is no rayformer. But Willum J. undherstands that there's a few hundherds iv thousands iv people livin' in a part iv th' town that looks like nawthin' but smoke fr'm th' roof iv th' Onion League Club that have on'y two pleasures in life, to wur-ruk an' to vote, both iv which they do at th' uniform rate iv wan dollar an' a half a day. That's why Willum J. O'Brien is now a sinitor an' will be an aldherman afther next Thursdah, an' it's why other people are sindin' him flowers.

"This is th' way a rayform candydate is ilicted. Th' boys down town has heerd that things ain't goin' r-right somehow. Franchises is bein' handed out to none iv thim; an' wanst in a while a mimber iv th' club, comin' home a little late an' thryin' to riconcile a pair iv r-round feet with an embroidered sidewalk, meets a sthrong ar-rm boy that pushes in his face an' takes away all his marbles. It begins to be talked that th' time has come f'r good citizens f'r to brace up an' do somethin', an' they agree to nomynate a candydate f'r aldherman. 'Who'll we put up?' says they. 'How's Clarence Doolittle?' says wan. 'He's laid up with a coupon thumb, an' can't r-run.' 'An' how about Arthur Doheny?' 'I swore an oath whin I came out iv colledge I'd niver vote f'r a man that wore a made tie.' 'Well, thin, let's thry Willie Boye.' 'Good,' says th' comity. 'He's jus' th' man f'r our money.' An' Willie Boye, after thinkin' it over, goes to his tailor an' ordhers three dozen pairs iv pants, an' decides f'r to be th' sthandard-bearer iv th' people. Musin' over his fried eyesthers an' asparagus an' his champagne, he bets a polo pony again a box of golf-balls he'll be ilicted unanimous; an' all th' good citizens make a vow f'r to set th' alar-rm clock f'r half-past three on th' afthernoon iv iliction day, so's to be up in time to vote f'r th' riprisintitive iv pure gover'mint.

" 'Tis some time befure they comprehind that there ar-re other candydates in th' field. But th' other candydates know it. Th' sthrongest iv thim—his name is Flannigan, an' he's a re-tail dealer in wines an' liquors, an' he lives over his establishment. Flannigan was nomynated enthusyastically at a prim'ry held in his bar-rn; an' befure Willie Boye had picked out pants that wud match th' color iv th' Austhreelyan ballot this here Flannigan had put a man on th' day watch, tol' him to speak gently to anny raygistered voter that wint to sleep behind th' sthove, an' was out that night visitin' his frinds. Who was it judged th' cake walk? Flannigan. Who was it carrid th' pall? Flannigan. Who was it sthud up at th' christening? Flannigan. Whose ca-ards did th' grievin' widow, th' blushin' bridegroom, or th' happy father find in th' hack? Flannigan's. Ye bet ye'er life. Ye see Flannigan wasn't out f'r th' good iv th' community. Flannigan was out f'r Flannigan an' th' stuff.

"Well, iliction day come around; an' all th' imminent frinds iv good gover'mint had special wires sthrung into th' club, an' waited f'r th' returns. Th' first precin't showed 28 votes f'r Willie Boye to 14 f'r Flannigan. 'That's my precin't,' says Willie. 'I wondher who voted thim fourteen?' 'Coachmen,' says Clarence Doolittle. 'There are thirty-five precin'ts in this ward,' says th' leader iv th' rayform ilimint. 'At this rate, I'm sure iv 440 meejority. Gossoon,' he says, 'put a ket iv sherry wine on th' ice,' he says. 'Well,' he says, 'at last th' community is relieved fr'm misrule,' he says. 'To-morrah I will start in arrangin' amindmints to th' tariff schedool an' th' ar-bitration threety,' he says. 'We must be up an' doin',' he says. 'Hol' on there,' says wan iv th' comity. 'There must be some mistake in this fr'm th' sixth precin't,' he says. 'Where's the sixth precin't?' says Clarence. 'Over be th' dumps,' says Willie. 'I told me futman to see to that. He lives at th' cor-ner iv Desplaines an Bloo Island Av'noo on Goose's Island,' he says. 'What does it show?' 'Flannigan, three hundherd an' eighty-five; Hansen, forty-eight; Schwartz, twinty; O'Malley, sivinteen; Casey, ten; O'Day, eight; Larsen, five; O'Rourke, three; Mulcahy, two; Schmitt, two; Moloney, two; Riordon, two; O'Malley, two; Willie Boye, wan.' 'Gintlemin,' says Willie Boye, arisin' with a stern look in his eyes, 'th' rascal has bethrayed me. Waither, take th' sherry wine off th' ice. They'se no hope f'r sound financial legislation this year. I'm goin' home.'

"An', as he goes down th' sthreet, he hears a band play an' sees a procission headed be a calceem light; an', in a carredge, with his plug hat in his hand an' his di'mond makin' th' calceem look like a piece iv punk in a smoke-house, is Flannigan, payin' his first visit this side iv th' thracks."

On Paternal Duty

"I'M havin' a time iv it with Terence," said Mr. Hennessy, despondently.

"What's th' la-ad been doin'?" asked Mr. Dooley.

"It ain't so much what he's doin'," Mr. Hennessy explained, "as what he ain't doin.' He ain't stayin' home iv nights, an' he ain't wurrukin'; but he does be out on th' corner with th' Cromleys an' th' rest, dancin' jig steps an' whistlin' th' 'Rogue's March' whin a polisman goes by. Sure, I can do nawthin' with him, f'r he's that kind an' good at home that he'd melt th' heart iv a man iv stone. But it's gray me life is, thinkin' iv what's to become iv him whin he gets to be a man grown. Ye're lucky, Martin, that ye're childless."

"Sure, I cudden't be anny other way, an' hold me good name," said Mr. Dooley. "An', whin I look about me sometimes, it's glad I am. They'se been times, perhaps—But lave that go. Is there somethin' in th' air or is it in oursilves that makes th' childher nowadays turn out to curse th' lives iv thim that give thim life? It may be in th' thrainin'. Whin I was a kid, they were brought up to love, honor, an' respect th' ol' folks, that their days might be long in th' land. Amen. If they didn't, th' best they cud do was to say nawthin' about it. 'Twas th' back iv th' hand an' th' sowl iv th' fut to th' la-ad that put his spoon first into th' stirabout. Between th' whalin's we got at school h'isted on th' back iv th' big boy that was bein' thrainned to be a Christyan brother an'

71

th' thumpin's we got at home, we was kept sore an' sthraight fr'm wan year's end to another. 'Twas no mild doses they give us, ayether. I mind wanst, whin I was near as big as I am now, I handed back some onkind re-emarks to me poor father that's dead. May he rest in peace, per Dominum! He must iv been a small man, an' bent with wurruk an' worry. But did he take me jaw? He did not. He hauled off, an' give me a r-right hook where th' bad wurruds come fr'm. I put up a pretty fight, f'r me years; but th' man doesn't live that can lick his own father. He rowled me acrost an oat-field, an' I give up. I didn't love him anny too well f'r that lickin', but I respected him; an', if he'd come into this place to-night, — an' he'd be near a hundherd: he was born in th' year '98, an' pikes was hid in his cradle, — if he come in here to-night an' pulled me ear, I'd fear to go again him. I wud so.

" 'Tis th' other way about now. Did ye iver know a man be th' name iv Ahearn? Ye did not? Well, maybe he was befure yer time. He was a cobbler be thrade; but he picked up money be livin' off iv leather findings an' wooden pegs, an' bought pieces iv th' prairie, an' starved an' bought more, an' starved an' starved till his heart was shrivelled up like a washerwoman's hand. But he made money. An' th' more he made, th' more he wanted, an', wantin' nawthin' more, it come to him fr'm th' divvle, who kept th' curse f'r his own time. This man Ahearn, whin he had acres an' acres on Halsted Sthreet, an' tinants be th' scoor that prayed at nights f'r him that he might live long an' taste sorrow, he marrid a girl. Her name was Ryan, a little, scared, foolish woman; an' she died whin a boy was bor-rn. Adhearn give her a solemn rayqueem high mass an' a monument at Calv'ry that ye can see fr'm th' fun'ral thrain. An' he come fr'm th' fun'ral with th' first smile on his face that anny man iver see there, an' th' baby in his ar-rms.

"I'll not say Ahearn was a changed man. Th' love iv money was knitted into his heart; an', afther th' la-ad come, th' way he ground th' people that lived in his house was death an' destruction. 'I must provide f'r me own,' he said. But thim that was kind to th' kid cud break th' crust, an' all th' r-rough, hard-wurrkin' tenants paid f'r th' favors he give to th' ol' frauds an' beguilin' women that petted Dan'l O'Connell Ahearn. Nawthin'

was too good f'r th' kid. He had nurses an' servants to wait on
him. He had clothes that'd stock this ba-ar f'r a year. Whin he
was old enough, he was sint to Saint Ignatyous. An' th' ol' man'd
take him walkin' on a Sundah, an' pint out th' rows an' rows iv
houses, with th' childher in front gazin' in awe at th' great man
an' their fathers glowerin' fr'm the windows, an' say, 'Thim will
all be yours whin ye grow up, Dan'l O'Connell, avick.'

"Well, it didn't take an eye iv a witch to see that Dan'l
O'Connell was a bor-rn idjet. They was no rale harm in th' poor
la-ad, on'y he was lazy an' foolish an' sort iv tired like. To make
a long story short, Hinnissy, his father thried ivrything f'r him,
an' got nawthin.' He didn't dhrink much, he cared little f'r
women, he liked to play ca-ards, but not f'r money. He did
nawthin' that was bad; an' yet he was no good at all, at all, —
just a slow, tired, aisy-goin', shamblin' la-ad, — th' sort that'd
wrench th' heart iv a father like Ahearn. I dinnaw what he did
fin'lly, but wan night he come into my place an' said he'd been
turned out be his father an' wanted a place f'r to sleep. 'Ye'll
sleep at home,' says I. 'Ye'er father sh'd take shame to himsilf, —
him a rich man.' An' I put on me coat, an' wint over to Ahearn's.
I was a power in th' wa-ard in thim days, an' feared no man
alive. Th' ol' la-ad met us at th' dure. Whin I started to speak,
he blazed up. 'Misther Dooley,' says he, 'my sorros are me own.
I'll keep thim here. As f'r ye,' he says, an' tur-rned like a tiger
on th' boy an' sthruck him with his ol' leathery hand. Th' boy
stood f'r a minnyit, an' thin walked out, me with him. I niver
see him since. We left Ahearn standin' there, as we used to say
iv th' fox in th' ol' counthry, cornered between th' river an' th'
wall."

"Ye're lucky to be alone," said Mr. Hennessy as he left.

"I think so," said Mr. Dooley. But there was no content upon
his face as he watched a lounging oaf of a boy catch up with
Mr. Hennessy, exchange a curtly affectionate greeting, and walk
over to where Mrs. Hennessy could be seen reading the "Key
of Heaven" beside the parlor stove.

On Criminals

"LORD bless my sowl," said Mr. Dooley, "childher is a gr-reat risponsibility,—a gr-reat risponsibility. Whin I think iv it, I praise th' saints I niver was married, though I had opporchunities enough whin I was a young man; an' even now I have to wear me hat low whin I go down be Cologne Sthreet on account iv th' Widow Grogan. Jawn, that woman'll take me dead or alive. I wake up in a col' chill in th' middle iv th' night, dhreamin' iv her havin' me in her clutches.

"But that's not here or there, avick. I was r-readin' in th' pa-apers iv a lad be th' name iv Scanlan bein' sint down th' short r-road f'r near a lifetime; an' I minded th' first time I iver see him,—a bit iv a curly-haired boy that played tag around me place, an' 'd sing 'Blest Saint Joseph' with a smile on his face like an angel's. Who'll tell what makes wan man a thief an' another man a saint? I dinnaw. This here boy's father wurrked fr'm morn till night in th' mills, was at early mass Sundah mornin' befure th' alkalis lit th' candles, an' niver knowed a month whin he failed his jooty. An' his mother was a sweet-faced little woman, though fr'm th' County Kerry, that nursed th' sick an' waked th' dead, an' niver had a hard thought in her simple mind f'r anny iv Gawd's creatures. Poor sowl, she's dead now. May she rest in peace!

"He didn't git th' shtreak fr'm his father or fr'm his mother. His brothers an' sisters was as fine a lot as iver lived. But this

74

la-ad Petey Scanlan growed up fr'm bein' a curly-haired angel f'r to be th' toughest villyun in th' r-road. What was it at all, at all? Sometimes I think they'se poison in th' life iv a big city. Th' flowers won't grow here no more thin they wud in a tannery, an' th' bur-rds have no song; an' th' childher iv dacint men an' women come up hard in th' mouth an' with their hands raised again their kind.

"Th' la-ad was th' scoorge iv th' polis. He was as quick as a cat an' as fierce as a tiger, an' I well raymimber him havin' laid out big Kelly that used to thravel this post, — 'Whistlin'' Kelly that kep' us awake with imitations iv a mockin' bur-rd, — I well raymimber him scuttlin' up th' alley with a score iv polismin laborin' afther him, thryin' f'r a shot at him as he wint around th' bar-rns or undher th' thrucks. He slep' in th' coalsheds afther that until th' poor ol' man cud square it with th' loot. But, whin he come out, ye cud see how his face had hardened an' his ways changed. He was as silent as an animal, with a sideways manner that watched ivrything. Right here in this place I seen him stand f'r a quarther iv an' hour, not seemin' to hear a dhrunk man abusin' him, an' thin lep out like a snake. We had to pry him loose.

"Th' ol' folks done th' best they cud with him. They hauled him out iv station an' jail an' bridewell. Wanst in a long while they'd dhrag him off to church with his head down: that was always afther he'd been sloughed up f'r wan thing or another. Between times th' polis give him his own side iv th' sthreet, an' on'y took him whin his back was tur-rned. Thin he'd go in the wagon with a mountain iv thim on top iv him, swayin' an' swearin' an' sthrikin' each other in their hurry to put him to sleep with their clubs.

"I mind well th' time he was first took to be settled f'r good. I heerd a noise in th' ya-ard, an' thin he come through th' place with his face dead gray an' his lips just a turn grayer. 'Where ar-re ye goin', Petey?' says I. 'I was jus' takin' a short cut home,' he says. In three minyits th' r-road was full iv polismin. They'd been a robbery down in Halsted Sthreet. A man that had a grocery sthore was stuck up, an' whin he fought was clubbed near to death; an' they'd r-run Scanlan through th' alleys to his father's house. That was as far as they'd go. They was enough iv thim to've kicked down th' little cottage with their heavy boots, but they knew he was standin' behind th' dure with th' big gun in his hand; an', though they was manny a good lad there, they was none that cared f'r that short odds.

"They talked an' palavered outside, an' telephoned th' chief iv polis, an' more pathrol wagons come up. Some was f'r settin' fire to th' buildin', but no wan moved ahead. Thin th' fr-ront dure opened, an' who shud come out but th' little mother. She was thin an' pale, an' she had her apron in her hands, pluckin' at it. 'Gintlemin,' she says, 'what is it ye want iv me?' she says. 'Liftinant Cassidy,' she says, "tis sthrange f'r ye that I've knowed so long to make scandal iv me befure me neighbors,' she says. 'Mrs. Scanlan,' says he, 'we want th' boy. I'm sorry, ma'am, but he's mixed up in a bad scrape, an' we must have him,' he says. She made a curtsy to thim, an' wint indures. 'Twas less than a minyit befure she come out, clingin' to th' la-ad's ar-rm. 'He'll go,' she says. 'Thanks be, though he's wild, they'se no crime on his head. Is there, dear?' 'No,' says he, like th' game kid he is. Wan iv th' polismin stharted to take hold iv him, but th' la-ad pushed him back; an' he wint to th' wagon on his mother's ar-rm."

"And was he really innocent?" Mrs. McKenna asked.

"No," said Mr. Dooley. "But she niver knowed it. Th' ol' man come home an' found her: she was settin' in a big chair with her apron in her hands an th' picture iv th' la-ad in her lap."

On a Plot

"WELL," said Mr. Dooley, "th' European situation is becomin' a little gay."

"It 'tis so," said Mr. Hennessy. "If I was conthrollin' anny iv the gr-reat powers, I'd go down to th' Phosphorus an' take th' sultan be th' back iv th' neck an' give him wan, two, three. 'Tis a shame f'r him to be desthroyin' white people without anny man layin' hands on him. Th' man's no frind iv mine. He ought to be impeached an' thrun out."

"Divvle take th' sultan," said Mr. Dooley. "It's little I care f'r him or th' likes iv him or th' Ar-menyans or th' Phosphorus. I was runnin' over in me mind about th' poor lads they have sloughed up beyant f'r attimptin' to blow up Queen Victorya an' th cza-ar iv Rooshia. Glory be, but they'se nawthin' in the wide wurruld as aisy to undherstand as a rivoluchonary plot be our own people. You'll see a lad iv th' right sort that'd niver open his head fr'm wan end iv th' year to th' other; but, whin he's picked out to go on a mission to London, he niver laves off talkin' till they put him aboord th' steamer. Here was Tynan. They say he had a hand in sindin' Lord Cavendish down th' toboggan, though I'd not thrust his own tellin' as far as th' len'th iv me ar-rm. Now he figured out that th' thrue way to free Ireland was to go over an' blow th' windows in Winzer Palace, an' incidentally to hist th' queen an' th' Rooshian cza-ar without th' aid iv th' elevator. What this here Tynan had again th'

Rooshian cza-ar I niver heerd. But 'twas something awful, ye may be sure.

"Well, th' first thing th' la-ads done was to go to Madison Square Garden an' hold a secret meetin', in which thim that was to hand th' package to th' queen and thim that was to toss a piece iv gas pipe to his cza-ars was told off. Thin a comity was sint around to th' newspaper offices to tell thim th' expedition was about to start. Th' conspirators, heavily disgeesed, was attinded to th' boat be a long procission. First come Tynan ridin' on a wagon-load iv nithroglycerine; thin th' other conspirators, with gas-pipe bombs an' picks an' chuvvels f'r tunnellin' undher Winzer Castle; thin th' Ah-o-haitches; thin th' raypoorthers; thin a brigade iv Scotland Ya-ard spies in th' ga-arb iv polismin. An' so off they wint on their secret mission, with th' band playin' 'Th' Wearin' iv th' Green,' and Tynan standin' on th' quarther deck, smilin' an' bowin' an' wavin' a bag iv jint powdher over his head.

"No sooner had th' conspirators landed thin th' British gover'mint begun to grow suspicious iv thim. Tynan was shadowed be detectives in citizens' clothes; an', whin he was seen out in his backyard practisin' blowin' up a bar'l that he'd dhressed in a shawl an' a little lace cap, th' suspicions growed. Ivrywhere that Tynan wint he was purshooed be th' minions iv tyranny. Whin he visited th' house nex' dure to th' queen's, an' unloaded a dhray full iv explosives an' chuvvels, the fact was rayported to th' polis, who become exthremely vigilant. Th' detectives followed him to Scotland Yard, where he wint to inform th' captain iv th' conspiracy, an' overheard much damming ividence iv th' plot until they become more an' more suspicious that something was on, although what was th' intintions iv th' conspirators it was hard to make out fr'm their peculiar actions. Whin Tynan gathered his followers in Hyde Park, an' notified thim iv the positions they was to take and disthributed th' dinnymite among thim, th' detectives become decidedly suspicious. Their suspicions was again aroused whin Tynan asked permission iv th' common council to build a bay window up close to th' queen's bedroom. But th' time to act had not come, an' they continted thimselves with thrackin' him through th' sthreets an' takin' notes iv such suspicious remarks as 'Anny wan that wants mememtoes iv th' queen has on'y to be around this neighborhood nex' week with a shovel an' a basket,' an' 'Onless ye want ye'er clothes to be spoiled be th' czar, ye'd best carry umbrellas.' On th' followin' day Tynan took th' step that was needed f'r to con-vince th' gover'mint that he had designs on the monarchs. He wint to France. It's always been obsarved that, whin a dinnymiter had to blow up annything in London, he laves th' counthry. Th' polis, now thoroughly aroused, acted with commindable prompt-ness. They arristed Tynan in Booloon f'r th' murdher iv Cav-endish.

"Thus," said Mr. Dooley, sadly, "thus is th' vengeance f'r which our beloved counthry has awaited so long delayed be th' hand iv onscrupulious tyranny. Sthrive as our heroes may, no secrecy is secure against th' corruption iv British goold. Oh, Ireland, is this to be thy fate forever? Ar-re ye niver to escape th' vigilance iv th' polis, thim cold-eyed sleuths that seem to read th' very thoughts iv ye'er pathriot sons?"

"There must have been a spy in th' ranks," said Mr. Hennessy.

"Sure thing," said Mr. Dooley, winking at Mr. McKenna. "Sure thing, Hinnissy. Ayether that or th' accomplished detictives at Scotland Yards keep a close watch iv the newspapers. Or it may be—who knows?—that Tynan was indiscreet. He may have dhropped a hint of his intintions."

On the New Woman

"MOLLIE DONAHUE have up an' become a new woman!

"It's been a good thing f'r ol' man Donahue, though, Jawn. He shtud ivrything that mortal man cud stand. He seen her appearin' in th' road wearin' clothes that no lady shud wear an' ridin' a bicycle; he was humiliated whin she demanded to vote; he put his pride under his ar-rm an' ma-arched out iv th' house whin she committed assault-an'-batthry on th' piannah. But he's got to th' end iv th' rope now. He was in here las' night, how-come-ye-so, with his hat cocked over his eye an' a look iv riso-lution on his face; an' whin he left me, he says, says he, 'Dooley,' he says, 'I'll conquir, or I'll die,' he says.

"It's been comin f'r months, but it on'y bust on Donahue las' week. He'd come home at night tired out, an' afther supper he was pullin' off his boots, whin Mollie an' th' mother begun talkin' about th' rights iv females. ''Tis th' era iv th' new woman,' says Mollie. 'Ye're right,' says th' mother. 'What d'ye mean be the new woman?' says Donahue, holdin' his boot in his hand. 'Th' new woman,' says Mollie, ''ll be free fr'm th' opprision iv man,' she says. 'She'll wurruk out her own way, without help or hind-erance,' she says. 'She'll wear what clothes she wants,' she says, 'an' she'll be no man's slave,' she says. 'They'll be no such thing as givin' a girl in marredge to a clown an' makin' her dipindant on his whims,' she says. 'Th' women'll earn their own livin',' she says; 'an' mebbe,' she says, 'th' men'll stay at home an' dredge in th' house wurruk,' she says. 'A-ho,' says Donahue. 'An' that's th' new woman, is it?' he says. An' he said no more that night.

"But th' nex' mornin' Mrs. Donahue an' Mollie come to his dure. 'Get up,' says Mrs. Donahue, 'an' bring in some coal,' she says. 'Ye drowsy man, ye'll be late f'r ye'er wurruk.' 'Divvle th' bit iv coal I'll fetch,' says Donahue. 'Go away an' lave me alone,' he says. 'Ye're inthruptin' me dreams.' 'What ails ye, man alive?' says Mrs. Donahue. 'Get up.' 'Go away,' says Donahue, 'an lave me slumber,' he says. 'Th' idee iv a couple iv big strong women like you makin' me wurruk f'r ye,' he says. 'Mollie 'll bring in th' coal,' he says. 'An' as f'r you Honoria, ye'd best see what there is in th' cupboord an' put it in ye'er dinner-pail,' he says. 'I heerd th' first whistle blow a minyit ago,' he says; 'an' there's a pile iv slag at th' mills that has to be wheeled off befure th' sup'rintindint comes around,' he says. 'Ye know ye can't afford to lose ye'er job with me in this dilicate condition,' he says. 'I'm going to sleep now,' he says. 'An', Mollie, do ye bring me in a cup iv cocoa an' a pooched igg at tin,' he says. 'I ixpect me music-teacher about that time. We have to take a wallop out iv Wagner an' Bootoven befure noon.' 'Th' Lord save us fr'm harm,' says Mrs. Donahue. 'Th' man's clean crazy.' 'Divvle's th' bit,' says Donahue, wavin' his red flannel undhershirt in th' air. 'I'm the new man,' he says.

"Well, sir, Donahue said it flured thim complete. They didn't know what to say. Mollie was game, an' she fetched in th' coal; but Mrs. Donahue got nervous as eight o'clock come around. 'Ye're not goin' to stay in bed all day an' lose ye'er job,' she says. 'Th' 'ell with me job,' says Donahue. 'I'm not th' man to take wurruk whin they'se industhrees women with nawthin' to do,' he says. 'Show me th' pa-apers,' he says. 'I want to see where I can get an eighty-cint bonnet f'r two and a half.' He's that stubborn he'd've stayed in bed all day, but th' good woman weakened. 'Come,' she says, 'don't be foolish,' she says. 'Ye wudden't have th' ol' woman wurrukin' in th' mills,' she says. ''Twas all a joke,' she says. 'Oh-ho, th' ol' woman!' he says. 'Th' ol' woman! Well, that's a horse iv another color,' he says. 'An' I don't mind tellin' ye th' mills is closed down to-day, Honoria.' So he dhressed himsilf an' wint out; an' says he to Mollie, he says: 'Miss Newwoman,' says he, 'ye may find wurruk enough around th' house,' he says. 'An', if ye have time, ye might paint th' stoop,' he says. 'Th' ol' man is goin' to take th' ol' woman down be Halsted Sthreet' an' blow himsilf f'r a new shawl f'r her.'

"An' he's been that proud iv th' victhry that he's been a reg'lar customer f'r a week."

On Expert Testimony

"ANNYTHING new?" said Mr. Hennessy, who had been waiting patiently for Mr. Dooley to put down his newspaper.

"I've been r-readin' th' tistimony iv th' Lootgert case," said Mr. Dooley.

"What d'ye think iv it?"

"I think so," said Mr. Dooley.

"Think what?"

"How do I know?" said Mr. Dooley. "How do I know what I think? I'm no combi-nation iv chemist, doctor, osteologist, polisman, an' sausage-maker, that I can give ye an opinion right off th' bat. A man needs to be all iv thim things to detarmine annything about a murdher trile in these days. This shows how intilligent our methods is, as Hogan says. A large German man is charged with puttin' his wife away into a breakfas'-dish, an' he says he didn't do it. Th' on'y question, thin, is, Did or did not Alphonse Lootgert stick Mrs. L. into a vat, an' rayjooce her to a quick lunch? Am I right?"

"Ye ar-rè," said Mr. Hennessy.

"That's simple enough. What th' coort ought to've done was to call him up, an' say: 'Lootgert, where's ye'er good woman?' If Lootgert cudden't tell, he ought to be hanged on gin'ral principles; f'r a man must keep his wife around th' house, an' whin she isn't there, it shows he's a poor provider. But, if Lootgert says, 'I don't know where me wife is,' the coort shud say:

'Go out, an' find her. If ye can't projooce her in a week, I'll fix ye.' An' let that be th' end iv it.

"But what do they do? They get Lootgert into coort an' stand him up befure a gang iv young rayporthers an' th' likes iv thim to make pitchers iv him. Thin they summon a jury composed iv poor tired, sleepy expressmen an' tailors an' clerks. Thin they call in a profissor from a colledge. 'Profissor,' says th' lawyer f'r the State, 'I put it to ye if a wooden vat three hundherd an' sixty feet long, twenty-eight feet deep, an' sivinty-five feet wide, an' if three hundherd pounds iv caustic soda boiled, an' if the leg iv a guinea pig, an' ye said yestherdah about bi-carbonate iv soda, an' if it washes up an' washes over, an' th' slimy, slippery stuff, an' if a false tooth or a lock iv hair or a jawbone or a goluf ball across th' cellar eleven feet nine inches—that is, two inches this way an' five gallons that?' 'I agree with ye intirely,' says th' profissor. 'I made lab'ratory experiments in an' ir'n basin, with bichloride iv gool, which I will call soup-stock, an' coal tar, which I will call ir'n filings. I mixed th' two over a hot fire, an' left in a cool place to harden. I thin packed it in ice, which I will call glue, an' rock-salt, which I will call fried eggs, an' obtained a dark, queer solution that is a cure f'r freckles, which I will call antimony or doughnuts or annything I blamed please.'

" 'But,' says th' lawyer f'r th' State, 'measurin' th' vat with gas,—an' I lave it to ye whether this is not th' on'y fair test,—an' supposin' that two feet acrost is akel to tin feet sideways, an' supposin' that a thick green an' hard substance, an' I daresay it wud; an' supposin' you may, takin' into account th' measure-mints,—twelve be eight,—th' vat bein' wound with twine six inches fr'm th' handle an' a rub iv th' green, thin ar-re not human teeth often found in counthry sausage?' 'In th' winter,' says th' profissor. 'But th' sisymoid bone is sometimes seen in th' fut, sometimes worn as a watch-charm. I took two sisymoid bones, which I will call poker dice, an' shook thim together in a cylinder, which I will call Fido, poored in a can iv milk, which I will call gum arabic, took two pounds iv rough-on-rats, which I rayfuse to call; but th' raysult is th' same.' Question be th' coort: 'Different?' Answer: 'Yis.' Th' coort: 'Th' same.' Be Misther McEwen: 'Whose bones?' Answer: 'Yis.' Be Misther Vincent: 'Will ye go to th' divvle?' Answer: 'It dissolves th' hair.'

"Now what I want to know is where th' jury gets off. What has that collection iv pure-minded pathrites to larn fr'm this here polite discussion, where no wan is so crool as to ask what anny wan else means? Thank th' Lord, whin th' case is all over, the jury'll pitch th' tistimony out iv th' window, an' consider three questions: 'Did Lootgert look as though he'd kill his wife? Did his wife look as though she ought to be kilt? Isn't it time we wint to supper?' An', howiver they answer, they'll be right, an' it'll make little diff'rence wan way or th' other. Th' German vote is too large an' ignorant, annyhow."

On the Popularity of Firemen

"I KNOWED a man be th' name iv Clancy wanst, Jawn. He was fr'm th' County May-o, but a good man f'r all that; an', whin he'd growed to be a big, sthrappin' fellow, he wint on to th' fire departmint. They'se an Irishman 'r two on th' fire departmint an' in th' army, too, Jawn, though ye'd think be hearin' some talk they was all runnin' prim'ries an' thryin' to be cinthral comitymen. So ye wud. Ye niver hear iv thim on'y whin they die; an' thin, murther, what funerals they have!

"Well, this Clancy wint on th' fire departmint, an' they give him a place in thruck twenty-three. All th' r-road was proud iv him, an' faith he was proud iv himsilf. He r-rode free on th' sthreet ca-ars, an' was th' champeen hand-ball player f'r miles around. Ye shud see him goin' down th' sthreet, with his blue shirt an' his blue coat with th' buttons on it, an' his cap on his ear. But ne'er a cap or coat'd he wear whin they was a fire. He might be shiv'rin' be th' stove in th' ingine house with a buffalo robe over his head; but, whin th' gong sthruck, 'twas off with coat an' cap an' buffalo robe, an' out come me brave Clancy, bare-headed an' bare hand, dhrivin' with wan line an' spillin' th' hose cart on wan wheel at ivry jump iv th' horse. Did anny wan iver see a fireman with his coat on or a polisman with his off? Why, wanst, whin Clancy was standin' up f'r Grogan's eighth, his son come runnin' in to tell him they was a fire in Vogel's packin' house. He dhropped th' kid at Father Kelly's feet, an'

86

whipped off his long coat an' wint tearin' f'r th' dure, kickin' over th' poorbox an' buttin' ol' Mis' O'Neill that'd come in to say th' stations. 'Twas lucky 'twas wan iv th' Grogans. They're a fine family f'r falls. Jawn Grogan was wurrukin' on th' top iv Metzri an' O'Connell's brewery wanst, with a man be th' name iv Dorsey. He slipped an' fell wan hundherd feet. Whin they come to see if he was dead, he got up, an' says he: 'Lave me at him.' 'At who?' says they. 'He's deliryous,' they says. 'At Dorsey,' says Grogan. 'He thripped me.' So it didn't hurt Grogan's eighth to fall four 'r five feet.

"Well, Clancy wint to fires an' fires. Whin th' big organ facthry burnt, he carrid th' hose up to th' fourth story an' was squirtin' whin th' walls fell. They dug him out with pick an' shovel, an' he come up fr'm th' brick an' boards an' saluted th' chief. 'Clancy,' says th' chief, 'ye betther go over an' get a dhrink.' He did so, Jawn. I heerd it. An' Clancy was that proud!

"Whin th' Hogan flats on Halsted Sthreet took fire, they got all th' people out but wan; an' she was a woman asleep on th' fourth flure. 'Who'll go up?' says Bill Musham. 'Sure, sir,' says Clancy, 'I'll go'; an' up he wint. His captain was a man be th' name iv O'Connell, fr'm th' County Kerry; an' he had his fut on th' ladder whin Clancy started. Well, th' good man wint into th' smoke, with his wife faintin' down below. 'He'll be kilt,' says his brother. 'Ye don't know him,' says Bill Musham. An' sure enough, whin ivry wan'd give him up, out comes me brave Clancy, as black as a Turk, with th' girl in his arms. Th' others wint up like monkeys, but he shtud wavin' thim off, an' come down th' ladder face forward. 'Where'd ye larn that?' says Bill Musham. 'I seen a man do it at th' Lyceem whin I was a kid,' says Clancy. 'Was it all right?' 'I'll have ye up before th' ol' man,' says Bill Musham. 'I'll teach ye to come down a laddher as if ye was in a quadhrille, ye horse-stealin', ham-sthringin' May-o man,' he says. But he didn't. Clancy wint over to see his wife. 'O Mike,' says she, ''twas fine,' she says. 'But why d'ye take th' risk?' she says. 'Did ye see th' captain?' he says with a scowl. 'He wanted to go. Did ye think I'd follow a Kerry man with all th' ward lukkin' on?' he says.

"Well, so he wint dhrivin' th' hose-cart on wan wheel, an' jumpin' whin he heerd a man so much as hit a glass to make it

87

ring. All th' people looked up to him, an' th' kids followed him down th' sthreet; an' 'twas th' gr-reatest priv'lige f'r anny wan f'r to play dominos with him near th' joker. But about a year ago he come in to see me, an' says he, 'Well, I'm goin' to quit,' 'Why,' says I, 'ye-er a young man yet,' I says. 'Faith,' he says, 'look at me hair,' he says, — 'young heart, ol' head. I've been at it these twenty year, an' th' good woman's wantin' to see more iv me thin blowin' into a saucer iv coffee,' he says. 'I'm goin' to quit,' he says, 'on'y I want to see wan more good fire,' he says. 'A rale good ol' hot wan,' he says, 'with th' win' blowin' f'r it an' a good dhraft in th' ilivator-shaft, an' about two stories, with pitcher-frames an' gasoline an' excelsior, an' to hear th' chief yellin': "Play 'way, sivinteen. What th' hell an' damnation are ye standin' aroun' with that pipe f'r? Is this a fire 'r a dam livin' pitcher? I'll break ivry man iv eighteen, four, six, an' chem'cal five to-morrah mornin' befure breakfast." Oh,' he says, bringin' his fist down, 'wan more, an' I'll quit.'

"An' he did, Jawn. Th' day th' Carpenter Brothers' box factory burnt. 'Twas wan iv thim big, fine-lookin' buildings that pious men built out iv celluloid an' plasther iv Paris. An' Clancy was wan iv th' men undher whin th' wall fell. I see thim bringin' him home; an' th' little woman met him at th' dure, rumplin' her apron in her hands."

On the Game of Football

"Whin I was a young man," said Mr. Dooley, "an' that was a long time ago, — but not so long ago as manny iv me inimies'd like to believe, if I had anny inimies, — I played fut-ball, but 'twas not th' futball I see whin th' Brothers' school an' th' Saint Aloysius Tigers played las' week on th' pee-raries.

"Whin I was a la-ad, iv a Sundah afthernoon we'd get out in th' field where th' oats'd been cut away, an' we'd choose up sides. Wan cap'n'd pick one man, an' th' other another. 'I choose Dooley,' 'I choose O'Connor,' 'I choose Dimpsey,' 'I choose Rior- dan,' an' so on till there was twinty-five or thirty on a side. Thin wan cap'n'd kick th' ball, an' all our side'd r-run at it an' kick it back; an' thin wan iv th' other side'd kick it to us, an' afther awhile th' game'd get so timpischous that all th' la-ads iv both sides'd be in wan pile, kickin' away at wan or th' other or at th' ball or at th' impire, who was mos'ly a la-ad that cudden't play an' that come out less able to play thin he was whin he wint in. An', if anny wan laid hands on th' ball, he was kicked be ivry wan else an' be th' impire. We played fr'm noon till dark, an' kicked th' ball all th' way home in the moonlight.

"That was futball, an' I was a great wan to play it. I'd think nawthin' iv histin' th' ball two hundherd feet in th' air, an' wanst I give it such a boost that I stove in th' ribs iv th' Prowtestant minister — bad luck to him, he was a kind man — that was lookin' on fr'm a hedge. I was th' finest player in th' whole county, I was so.

"But this here game that I've been seein' ivry time th' pagan fistival iv Thanksgivin' comes ar-round, sure it ain't th' game I played. I seen th' Dorgan la-ad comin' up th' sthreet yesterdah in his futball clothes,—a pair iv matthresses on his legs, a pillow behind, a mask over his nose, an' a bushel measure iv hair on his head. He was followed by three men with bottles, Dr. Ryan, an' th' Dorgan fam'ly. I jined thim. They was a big crowd on th' peerary,—a bigger crowd than ye cud get to go f'r to see a prize fight. Both sides had their frinds that give th' colledge cries. Says wan crowd: 'Take an ax, an ax, an ax to thim. Hooroo, hooroo, hellabaloo. Christyan Bro-others!' an' th' other says, 'Hit thim, saw thim, gnaw thim, chaw thim, Saint Alo-ysius!' Well, afther awhile they got down to wur-ruk. 'Sivin, eighteen, two, four,' says a la-ad. I've seen people go mad over figures durin' th' free silver campaign, but I niver see figures make a man want f'r to go out an' kill his fellow-men befure. But these here figures had th' same effect on th' la-ads that amintion iv Lord Castle-reagh'd have on their fathers. Wan la-ad hauled off, an' give a la-ad acrost fr'm him a punch in th' stomach. His frind acrost th' way caught him in th' ear. Th' cinter rush iv th' Saint Aloy-siuses took a runnin' jump at th' left lung iv wan iv th' Christyan Brothers, an' wint to th' grass with him. Four Christyan Brothers leaped most crooly at four Saint Aloysiuses, an' rolled thim. Th' cap'n iv th' Saint Aloysiuses he took th' cap'n iv th' Christyan Brothers be th' leg, an' he pounded th' pile with him as I've seen a section hand tamp th' thrack. All this time young Dorgan was standin' back, takin' no hand in th' affray. All iv a suddent he give a cry iv rage, an' jumped feet foremost into th' pile. 'Down!' says th' impire. 'Faith, they are all iv that,' says I, 'Will iver they get up?' 'They will,' says ol' man Dorgan. 'Ye can't stop thim,' says he.

"It took some time f'r to pry thim off. Near ivry man iv th' Saint Aloysiuses was tied in a knot around wan iv th' Christyan Brothers. On'y wan iv them remained on th' field. He was lyin' face down, with his nose in th' mud. 'He's kilt,' says I. 'I think he is,' says Dorgan, with a merry smile. ''Twas my boy Jimmy done it, too,' says he. 'He'll be arrested f'r murdher,' says I. 'He will not,' says he. 'There's on'y wan polisman in town cud take him, an' he's down town doin' th' same f'r somebody,' he says. Well, they carried th' corpse to th' side, an' took th' ball out iv his stomach with a monkey wrinch, an' th' game was rayshumed. 'Sivin, sixteen, eight, eleven,' says Saint Aloysius; an' young Dorgan started to run down th' field. They was another young la-ad r-runnin' in fr-front iv Dorgan; an', as fast as wan iv th' Christyan Brothers come up an' got in th' way, this here young Saint Aloysius grabbed him be th' hair iv th' head an' th' sole iv th' fut, an' thrun him over his shoulder. 'What's that la-ad doin'?' says I. 'Interferin',' says he. 'I shud think he was,' says I, 'an' most impudent,' I says. ''Tis such interference as this,' I says, 'that breaks up fam'lies'; an' I come away.

" 'Tis a noble sport, an' I'm glad to see us Irish ar-re gettin' into it. Whin we larn it thruly, we'll teach thim colledge joods fr'm th' pie belt a thrick or two."

"We have already," said Mr. Hennessy. "They'se a team up in Wisconsin with a la-ad be th' name iv Jeremiah Riordan f'r cap'n, an' wan named Patsy O'Dea behind him. They come down here, an' bate th' la-ads fr'm th' Chicawgo Colledge down be th' Midway."

"Iv coorse, they did,' said Mr. Dooley. "Iv coorse, they did. An' they cud bate anny collection iv Baptists that iver come out iv a tank."

On the Necessity of Modesty
among the Rich

"I WONDHER," said Mr. Hennessy, "if thim Hadley-Markhams that's goin' to give th' ball is anny kin iv th' aldherman?"

"I doubt it," said Mr. Dooley. "I knowed all his folks. They're Monaghan people, an' I niver heerd iv thim marryin' into th' Hadleys, who come fr'm away beyant near th' Joynt's Causeway. What med ye think iv thim?"

"I was readin' about th' Prowtestant minister that give thim such a turnin' over th' other night," said Hennessy. Then the Philistine went on: "It looks to me as though th' man was wr-rong, an' th' Hadley-Markhams was right. Faith, th' more th' poor can get out iv th' r-rich, th' better f'r thim. I seen it put just r-right in th' paper th' other day. If these people didn't let go iv their coin here, they'd take it away with thim to Paris or West Baden, Indiana, an' spind it instid iv puttin' it in circulation amongst th' florists an' dhressmakers an' hackmen they'll have to hire. I believe in encouragin' th' rich to walk away fr'm their change. 'Tis gr-reat f'r business."

Mr. Dooley mused over this proposition some time before he said:—

"Years ago, whin I was a little bit iv a kid, hardly high enough to look into th' pot iv stirabout on th' peat fire, they was a rich landlord in our part iv Ireland; an' he ownded near half th' counthryside. His name was Dorsey,—Willum Edmund Fitzgerald Dorsey, justice iv th' peace, mimber iv Parlymint.

"I'll niver tell ye how much land that man had in his own r-right. Ye cud walk f'r a day without lavin' it, bog an' oat-field an' pasthure an' game presarves. He was smothered with money, an' he lived in a house as big as th' Audjitoroom Hotel. Manny's th' time I've seen him ride by our place, an' me father'd raise his head from th' kish iv turf an' touch his hat to th' gr-reat man. An' wanst or twict in th' month th' dogs'd come yelpin' acrost our little place, with lads follerin' afther in r-red coats; f'r this Dorsey was a gr-reat huntsman, bad scran to his evil face.

"He had th' r-reputation iv bein' a good landlord so long as th' crops come regular. He was vilent, it's thrue, an' 'd as lave as not cut a farmer acrost th' face with his whip f'r crossin' th' thrail iv th' fox; but he was liberal with his money, an', Hinnissy, that's a thrait that covers a multitude iv sins. He give freely to th' church, an' was as gin'rous to th' priest as to th' parson. He had th' gintry f'r miles around to his big house f'r balls an' dinners an' huntin' meetin's, an' half th' little shopkeepers in th' neighborin' town lived on th' money he spent f'r th' things he didn't bring fr'm Dublin or London. I mind wanst a great roar wint up whin he stayed th' whole season in England with his fam'ly. It near broke th' townsfolk, an' they were wild with delight whin he come back an' opened up th' big house.

"But wan year there come a flood iv rain, an' th nex' year another flood, an' th' third year there wasn't a lumper turned up that wasn't blue-black to th' hear-rt. We was betther off than most, an' we suffered our share, Gawd knows; but thim that was scrapin' th' sod f'r a bare livin' fr'm day to day perished like th' cattle in th' field.

"Thin come th' writs an' th' evictions. Th' bailiffs dhrove out in squads, seizin' cattle an' turnin' people into th' r-road. Nawthin' wud soften th' hear-rt iv Dorsey. I seen th' priest an' th' 'Piscopal ministher dhrivin' over to plead with him wan night; an' th' good man stopped at our house, comin' back, an' spent th' night with us. I heerd him tell me father what Dorsey said. 'Haven't I been lib'ral with me people?' he says. 'Haven't I give freely to ye'er churches? Haven't I put up soup-houses an' disthributed blankets whin th' weather was cold? Haven't I kept th' shopkeepers iv th' town beyant fr'm starvin' be thradin' with thim an' stayin' in this cur-rsed counthry, whin, if I'd done what me wife wanted, I'd been r-runnin' around Europe, enj'yin' life? I'm a risidint landlord. I ain't like Kilduff, that laves his estate in th' hands iv an agint. I'm proud iv me station. I was bor-rn here, an' here I'll die; but I'll have me r-rights. These here people owes their rent, an' I'll get th' rent or th' farms if I have to call on ivry rig'mint fr'm Bombay to Cape Clear, an' turn ivry oat-field into a pasture f'r me cattle. I stand on th' law. I'm a just man, an' I ask no more thin what belongs to me.'

"Ivry night they was a party on th' hill, an' th' people come fr'm miles around; an' th' tinants trudgin' over th' muddy roads with th' peelers behind thim cud see th' light poorin' out fr'm th' big house an' hear Devine's band playin' to th' dancers. Th' shopkeepers lived in clover, an' thanked th' lord f'r a good landlord, an' wan that lived at home. But one avnin' a black man be th' name iv Shaughnessy, that had thramped acrost th' hills fr'm Galway just in time to rent f'r th' potato rot, wint and hid himself in a hedge along th' road with a shotgun loaded with hardware under his coat. Dorsey'd heerd talk iv the people bein' aggrieved at him givin' big parties while his bailiffs were hustlin' men and women off their holdin's; but he was a high-handed man, an' foolish in his pride, an' he'd have it no other way but that he'd go about without protection. This night he rode alongside th' carredge iv some iv his frinds goin' to th' other side iv town, an' come back alone in th' moonlight. Th' Irish ar-re poor marksmen, Hinnissy, except whin they fire in platoons; but that big man loomin' up in th' moonlight on a black horse cud no more be missed thin th' r-rock iv Cashel. He niver knowed what hit him; an' Pether th' Packer come down th' followin' month, an' a jury iv shopkeepers hanged Shaughnessy so fast it med even th' judge smile."

"Well," said Mr. Hennessy, "I suppose he desarved it; but, if I'd been on th' jury, I'd've starved to death befure I'd give th' verdict."

"Thrue," said Mr. Dooley. "An' Dorsey was a fool. He might've evicted twinty thousan' tinants, an' lived to joke about it over his bottle. 'Twas th' music iv th' band an' th' dancin' on th' hill an' th' lights th' Galway man seen whin he wint up th' muddy road with his babby in his arrums that done th' business f'r Dorsey."

On the Power of Love

" 'Twas this way," said Mr. Hennessy, sparring at Mr. Dooley. "Fitz led his right light on head, thin he stuck his thumb in Corbett's hear-rt, an' that was th' end iv th' fight an' iv Pompydour Jim. I tol' ye how it wud come out. Th' punch over th' hear-rt done th' business."

"Not at all," said Mr. Dooley. "Not at all. 'Twas Mrs. Fitzsimmons done th' business. Did ye see the pitcher iv that lady? Did ye? Well, 'twud've gone har-rd with th' lad if he'd lost th' fight in th' ring. He'd have to lose another at home. I'll bet five dollars that th' first lady iv th' land licks th' champeen without th' aid iv a stove lid. I know it.

"As me good frind, Jawn Sullivan, says, 'tis a great comfort to have little reminders iv home near by whin ye're fightin'. Jawn had none, poor lad; an' that accounts f'r th' way he wint down at last. Th' home infloo-ence is felt in ivry walk iv life. Whin Corbett was poundin' th' first jintleman iv th' land like a man shinglin' a roof, th' first lady iv th' land stood in th' corner, cheerin' on th' bruised an' bleedin' hero. 'Darlin'' she says, 'think iv ye'er home, me love. Think,' she says, 'iv our little child larnin' his caddychism in Rahway, New Jersey,' she says. 'Think iv th' love I bear ye,' she says, 'an' paste him,' she says, 'in th' slats. Don't hit him on th' jaw,' she says. 'He's well thrained there. But tuck ye'er lovin' hooks into his diseased an' achin' ribs,' she says. 'Ah, love!' she says, 'recall thim happy goolden days iv our

95

coortship, whin we walked th' counthry lane in th' light iv th' moon,' she says, 'an hurl yer maulies into his hoops,' she says. 'Hit him on th' slats!' An' Fitz looked over his shoulder an' seen her face, an' strange feelin's iv tendherness come over him; an' thinks he to himself: 'What is so good as th' love iv a pure woman? If I don't nail this large man, she'll prob'ly kick in me head.' An' with this sacred sintimint in his heart he wint over an' jolted Corbett wan over th' lathes that retired him to th' home f'r decayed actors.

" 'Twas woman's love that done it, Hinnissy. I'll make a bet with ye that, if th' first lady iv th' land had been in th' ring instead iv th' first jintleman, Corbett wudden't have lasted wan r-round. I'd like to have such a wife as that. I'd do th' cookin', an' lave th' fightin' to her. There ought to be more like her. Th' throuble with th' race we're bringin' up is that th' fair sect, as Shakespeare calls thim, lacks inthrest in their jooty to their husbands. It's th' business iv men to fight an' th' business iv their wives f'r to make thim fight. Ye may talk iv th' immyrality iv nailin' a man on th' jaw, but 'tis in this way on'y that th' wurruld increases in happiness an' th' race in strenth. Did ye see annywan th' other day that wasn't askin' to know how th' fight come out? They might say that they re-garded th' exhibition as brutal an' disgustin', but divvle a wan iv thim but was waitin' around th' corner f'r th' rayturns, an' prayin' f'r wan or th' other iv th' big lads. Father Kelly mentioned th' scrap in his sermon last Sundah. He said it was a disgraceful an' corruptin' affair, an' he was ashamed to see th' young men iv th' parish takin' such an inthrest in it in Lent. But late Winsdah afthernoon he came bustlin' down th' sthreet. 'Nice day,' he says. It was poorin' rain. 'Fine,' says I. 'They was no parade to-day,' he says. 'No,' says I. 'Too bad,' says he; an' he started to go. Thin he turned, an' says he: 'Be th' way, how did that there foul an' outhrajous affray in Carson City come out?' 'Fitz,' says I, 'in th' fourteenth.' 'Ye don't say,' he says, dancin' around. 'Good,' he says. 'I told Father Doyle this mornin' at breakfuss that if that red-headed man iver got wan punch at th' other lad, I'd bet a new cassock—Oh, dear!' he says, 'what am I sayin'?' 'Ye're sayin',' says I, 'what nine-tenths iv th' people, laymen an' clargy, are sayin',' I says. 'Well,' he says, 'I guess ye're right,' he says. 'Afther all,' he says, 'an' undher all, we're mere brutes; an' it on'y takes two lads more brutal than th' rest f'r to expose th' sthreak in th' best iv us. Foorce rules th' wurruld, an' th' churches is empty whin th' blood begins to flow,' he says. 'It's too bad, too bad,' he says. 'Tell me, was Corbett much hurted?' he says."

On the Victorian Era

"AR-RE ye goin' to cillybrate th' queen's jubilee?" asked Mr. Dooley.

"What's that?" demanded Mr. Hennessy, with a violent start.

"To-day," said Mr. Dooley, "her gracious Majesty Victorya, Queen iv Great Britain an' that part iv Ireland north iv Sligo, has reigned f'r sixty long and tiresome years."

"I don't care if she has snowed f'r sixty years," said Mr. Hennessy. "I'll not cillybrate it. She may be a good woman f'r all I know, but dam her pollytics."

"Ye needn't be pro-fane about it," said Mr. Dooley. "I on'y ast ye a civil question. F'r mesilf, I have no feelin' on th' subject. I am not with th' queen an' I'm not again her. At th' same time I corjally agree with me frind Captain Finerty, who's put his newspaper in mournin' f'r th' ivint. I won't march in th' parade, an' I won't put anny dinnymite undher thim that does. I don't say th' marchers an' dinnymiters ar-re not both r-right. 'Tis purely a question iv taste, an', as the ixicutive says whin both candydates are mimbers iv th' camp, 'Pathrites will use their own discreetion.'

"Th' good woman niver done me no har-rm; an', beyond throwin' a rock or two into an orangey's procission an' subscribin' to tin dollars' worth iv Fenian bonds, I've threated her like a lady. Anny gredge I iver had again her I burrid long ago. We're both well on in years, an' 'tis no use carrying har-rd feelin's to th' grave. About th' time th' lord chamberlain wint over to tell her she was queen, an' she came out in her nitey to hear th' good news, I was announced into this wurruld iv sin an' sorrow. So ye see we've reigned about th' same lenth iv time, an' I ought to be cillybratin' me di'mon' jubilee. I wud, too, if I had anny di'mon's. Do ye r-run down to Aldherman O'Brien's an' borrow twinty or thirty f'r me.

"Great happenin's have me an' Queen Victorya seen in these sixty years. Durin' our binificent prisince on earth th' nations have grown r-rich an' prosperous. Great Britain has ixtinded her domain until th' sun niver sets on it. No more do th' original owners iv th' sile, they bein' kept movin' be th' polis. While she was lookin' on in England, I was lookin' on in this counthry. I have seen America spread out fr'm th' Atlantic to th' Pacific, with a branch office iv the Standard Ile Comp'ny in ivry hamlet. I've seen th' shackles dropped fr'm th' slave, so's he cud be lynched in Ohio. I've seen this gr-reat city desthroyed be fire fr'm De Koven Sthreet to th' Lake View pumpin' station, and thin rise felix-like fr'm its ashes, all but th' West Side, which was not burned. I've seen Jim Mace beat Mike McCool, an' Tom Allen beat Jim Mace, an' somebody beat Tom Allen, an' Jawn Sullivan beat him, an' Corbett beat Sullivan, an' Fitz beat Corbett; an', if I live to cillybrate me goold-watch-an'-chain jubilee, I may see some wan put it all over Fitz.

"Oh, what things I've seen in me day an' Victorya's! Think iv that gran' procission iv lithry men, — Tinnyson an' Longfellow an' Bill Nye an' Ella Wheeler Wilcox an' Tim Scanlan an' — an' I can't name thim all: they're too manny. An' th' brave gin'rals, — Von Molkey an' Bismarck an' U. S. Grant an' gallant Phil Shurdan an' Coxey. Think iv thim durin' me reign. An' th' invintions, — th' steam-injine an' th' printin'-press an' th' cotton-gin an' the gin sour an' th' bicycle an' th' flyin'-machine an' th' nickel-in-th'-slot machine an' th' Croker machine an' th' sody fountain an' — crownin' wur-ruk iv our civilization — th' cash raygisther. What gr-reat advances has science made in my time an' Victorya's! f'r, whin we entered public life, it took three men to watch th' bar-keep, while to-day ye can tell within eight dollars an hour what he's took in.

"Glory be, whin I look back fr'm this day iv gin'ral rejoicin' in me rhinestone jubilee, an' see what changes has taken place an' how manny people have died an' how much betther off th' wurruld is, I'm proud iv mesilf. War an' pest'lence an' famine have occurred in me time, but I count thim light compared with th' binifits that have fallen to th' race since I come on th' earth."

"What ar-re ye talkin' about?" cried Mr. Hennessy, in deep disgust. "All this time ye've been standin' behind this bar ladlin' out disturvbance to th' Sixth Wa-ard, an' ye haven't been as far east as Mitchigan Avnoo in twinty years. What have ye had to do with all these things?"

"Well," said Mr. Dooley, "I had as much to do with thim as th' queen."

On the Currency Question

"THERE'S some tough knots in this here currency question," said Mr. McKenna. "A lot of things I don't quite catch."

"Cough thim up," said Mr. Dooley. "I'm a reg'lar caddychism iv coinage. Who made ye? Gawd made me. Why did he make ye? F'r to know Him, love Him, an' sarve Him all me days. That's th' way iv th' caddychism I learned whin I was a la-ad behind a hedge; but now 'tis: Who made ye? Ladenburg, Thalman an' Comp'ny made me. Why did they make ye? F'r to know thim, love thim, an' sarve thim all me days. O-ho!"

"That's all r-right," said Mr. Thomas Larkin, the Kerry horse-shoer, who was leaning over the cigar-case, reading what Mr. Lincoln, Mr. Blaine, Mr. Edward Atkinson, and Mr. Andrew D. White had to say in a small pamphlet. "That's all r-right, Martin. But ye're talkin' like a Populist an' an anarchist an' a big bullhead gen'rally. Ye bring up two or three Jew men, an' think f'r to scare us with thim. But look here. Supposin' a man comes into my place an' lays down on th' anvil a silver dollar, an' I give it a wallop with me hammer"—

"Thin," said Mr. Dooley, "ye're knockin' th' gover'mint."

"How am I?" said Mr. Larkin. "Niver mind now: I take this here silver dollar, an' I fetch it wan with me hammer. What happens?"

"Th' man that give ye th' dollar hands ye wan in th' nose," said Mr. Dooley.

101

"Not at all, not at—all," said Mr. Larkin. "I take this here mutilated an' disfigured an' bum dollar down to th' three-asury, an' I hand it in' an' Carlisle says, 'What kind iv an ol' piece iv mud is this ye're flingin' at me?' he says. 'Take it away: it's nawthin' to me.' "

"True for you, Larkin," said Mr. McKenna. "You're on the right track. Carlisle couldn't take it after you'd smashed it."

"But," said Mr. Dooley, "look here: if ye had th' free an' unlimited coinage iv silver at a rat-io iv sixteen to wan, ye cud take this here mass iv silver down to Carlisle, an' say, 'Here, Jawn, give me a dollar'; an' he'd have to give it to ye."

"A dollar of what?" said Mr. McKenna.

"A dollar iv what?" repeated Mr. Dooley. "A dollar iv what? Man alive, don't ye know what a dollar is? Carlisle'd hand him out a plunk, a case, a buck. He'd say, 'Here, Larkin, ye're a dam fool to be mal-threatin' th' currincy iv yer adophted counthry, but I have to give ye a dollar because ye're a good fellow an' a frind iv Dooley's.' "

"He wouldn't say anything of the kind," said Mr. McKenna. "He'd give Larkin fifty cents."

"I'd push his face in if he did," said Mr. Larkin, warmly. "I'm as good a ma-an as he is anny day. I'll have no man rob me."

"But he wouldn't rob you," said Mr. McKenna. "Think of the purchasing power: you've got to always figure that out. A dollar you'd get then would be worth only half as much as it's worth now. It'd be a dollar like they run through the ringer down in Mexico."

"How can wan dollar be worth on'y half as much as another dollar, if they're both dollars an' th' man that made thim is at la-arge?" answered Mr. Dooley. "Here's a dollar, an' here's a dollar. Wan akels th' other. Now you take this here dollar, an' come into my place. 'Give me a brandy an' sody,' ye say. Thin what do I say?"

"You say you're just out of brandy and soda."

"So I do, so I do. Thin you ask f'r a little liquor with beer f'r a chaser. An' I give it to ye. Ye lay down wan iv these here quartz dollars. I return eighty-five cints. Larkin comes in later, ordhers th' same thing, an' I give him th' same threatment. I play no fav-rites. Entertainmint f'r man an' beast."

102

"But, if we had free silver, you'd charge thirty cents for the drink," said Mr. McKenna.

"I wud not," said Mr. Dooley, hotly. "I niver overcharged a man in my life, except durin' a campaign."

"No one accuses you of overcharging," explained Mr. McKenna. "Everybody would charge the same. It'd be the regular price."

"If it was," said Mr. Dooley, "they'd be a rivolution. But I don't believe it, Jawn. Let me tell ye wan thing. Whisky is th' standard iv value. It niver fluctuates; an' that's funny, too, seein' that so much iv it goes down. It was th' same price—fifteen cints a slug, two f'r a quarther—durin' the war; an' it was th' same price afther the war. The day befure th' crime iv sivinty-three it was worth fifteen cints: it was worth th' same th' day afther. Goold and silver fluctuates, up wan day, down another; but whisky stands firm an' strong, unchangeable as th' skies, immovable as a rock at fifteen or two f'r a quarther. If they want something solid as a standard iv value, something that niver is rajjooced in price, something ye can exchange f'r food an' other luxuries annywhere in th' civilized wurruld where man has a thirst, they'd move th' Mint over to th' internal rivinue office, and lave it stay there."

Both Mr. Larkin and Mr. McKenna were diverted by this fancy.

"There's some good argumints on both sides iv th' quisthion," said the Kerry man. "I heerd a man be th' name of Doyle, a helper, compare money to th' human lungs."

"Th' lung argumint is all right," said Mr. Dooley. "Th' whole currency question is a matther iv lungs."

On Political Parades

MR. HENNESSY, wearing a silver-painted stove-pipe hat and a silver cape and carrying a torch, came in, looking much the worse for wear. The hat was dented, the cape was torn, and there were marks on Mr. Hennessy's face.

"Where ye been?" asked Mr. Dooley.

"Ma-archin'," said Mr. Hennessy.

"Be th' looks iv ye, ye might have been th' line iv ma-arch f'r th' p'rade. Who's been doin' things to ye?"

"I had a currency debate with a man be th' name iv Joyce, a towny iv mine, in th' Audjiotoroom Hotel," said Mr. Hennessy. "Whin we got as far as th' price iv wheat in th' year iv th' big wind, we pushed each other. Give me a high glass iv beer. I'm as dhry as a gravel roof."

"Well," said Mr. Dooley, handing over the glass, "ye're an ol' man; an', as th' good book says, an ol' fool is th' worst yet. So I'll not thry to con-vince ye iv th' error iv ye'er ways. But why anny citizen that has things in his head shud dhress himself up like a sandwich-man, put a torch on his shoulder, an' toddle over this blessid town with his poor round feet, is more than I can come at with all me intelligence.

"I agree with ye perfectly, Hinnissy, that this here is a crisis in our histhry. On wan hand is arrayed th' Shylocks an' th' pathrites, an' on th' other side th' pathrites an' th' arnychists. Th' Constitution must be upheld, th' gover'mint must be main-

tained, th' down-throdden farmer an' workin' man must get
their rights. But do ye think, man alive, that ye're goin' to do
this be pourin' lard ile frim ye'er torch down ye'er spine or
thrippin' over sthreet-car tracks like a dhray-horse thryin' to play
circus? Is th' Constitution anny safer to-night because ye have
to have ye'er leg amputated to get ye'er boot off, or because
Joyce has made ye'er face look like th' back dure-step iv a German
resthrant?

"Jawnny Mack took me down in th' afthernoon f'r to see th'
monsthrous p'rade iv th' goold men. It was a gloryous spectacle.
Th' sthreets were crowded with goold bugs an' women an' polismin an' ambulances. Th' procission was miles an' miles long.
Labor an' capital marched side be side, or annyhow labor was
in its usual place, afther th' capitalists. It was a noble sight f'r
to see th' employer iv workin'men marchin' ahead iv his band
iv sturdy toilers that to rest thimsilves afther th' layboryous
occupations iv th' week was reelin' undher banners that dhrilled
a hole in their stomachs or carryin' two-be-fours joists to show
their allegance to th' naytional honor. A man that has to shovel
coke into a dhray or shove lumber out iv th' hole iv a barge or
elevate his profession be carryin' a hod iv mort to th' top iv a
laddher doesn't march with th' grace iv an antelope, be a blamed
sight. To march well, a man's feet have to be mates; an', if he
has two left feet both runnin' sideways, he ought to have interference boots to keep him fr'm settin' fire to his knees. Whin a
man walks as if he expected to lave a leg stuck in th' sthreet
behind him, he has th' gait proper f'r half-past six o'clock th'
avenin' befure pay-day. But 'tis not th' prance iv an American
citizen makin' a gloryous spectacle iv himsilf."

"They were coerced," said Mr. Hennessy, gloomily.

"Don't ye believe it," replied the philosopher. "It niver re-
quires coercion to get a man to make a monkey iv himsilf in a
prisidintial campaign. He does it as aisily as ye dhrink ye'er liquor,
an' that's too aisy. Don't ye believe thim lads with lumber
ya-ards on their necks an' bar'ls on their feet was coerced. There
wasn't wan iv thim that wudden't give his week's wages f'r a
chanst to show how many times he cud thrip over a manhole in
a mile. No more co-erced than ye are whin ye r-run down town
an' make an ape iv ye-ersilf. I see ye marchin' away fr'm Fin-

ucane's with th' Willum J. O'Briens. Th' man nex' to ye had a banner declarin' that he was no slave. 'Twas th' la-ad Johnson. He was r-right. He is no slave, an' he won't be wan as long as people have washin' to give to his wife. Th' man I see ye takin' a dhrink with had a banner that said if th' mines was opened th' mills would be opened, too. He meant be that, that if money was plenty enough f'r him to get some without wur-rukin', he'd open a gin mill. An' ye ma-arched afther Willum J. O'Brien, didn't ye? Well, he's a good la-ad. If I didn't think so, I wudden't say it until I got me strenth back or cud buy a gun. But did Willum J. O'Brien march? Not Willie. He was on horseback; an', Hinnissy, if dollars was made out iv Babbit metal, an' horses was worth sixty-sivin cints a dhrove, ye cudden't buy a crupper."

"Well," said Mr. Hennessy, "annyhow, I proved me hathred iv capital."

"So ye did," said Mr. Dooley. "So ye did. An' capital this afthernoon showed its hatred iv ye. Ye ought to match blisters to see which hates th' worst. Capital is at home now with his gams in a tub iv hot wather; an,' whin he comes down to-morrah to oppriss labor an' square his protisted notes, he'll have to go on all fours. As f'r you, Hinnissy, if 'twill aise ye anny, ye can hang f'r a few minyits fr'm th' gas fixtures. Did th' goold Dimmycrats have a p'rade?"

"No," said Mr. Hennessy. "But they rayviewed th' day procission fr'm th' Pammer House. Both iv thim was on th' stand."

106

On Charity

"BR-R-R!" cried Mr. McKenna, entering stiffly and spreading his hands over the pot-bellied stove. "It's cold."

"Where?" asked Mr. Dooley. "Not here."

"It's cold outside," said Mr. McKenna. "It was ten below at Shannahan's grocery when I went by, and the wind blowing like all possessed. Lord love us, but I pity them that's got to be out to-night."

"Save ye'er pity," said Mr. Dooley, comfortably. "It ain't cowld in here. There's frost on th' window, 'tis thrue for ye; an' th' wheels has been singin' th' livelong day. But what's that to us? Here I am, an' there ye are, th' stove between us an' th' kettle hummin'. In a minyit it'll bile, an' thin I'll give ye a taste iv what'll make a king iv ye.

"Well, tubby sure, 'tis thryin' to be dhrivin' a coal wagon or a sthreet-car; but 'tis all in a lifetime. Th' diff'rence between me an' th' man that sets up in th' seat thumpin' his chest with his hands is no more thin th' diff'rence between him an' th' poor divvle that walks along behind th' wagon with his shovel on his shoulder, an' 'll thank th' saints f'r th' first chanst to put tin ton iv ha-ard coal into a cellar f'r a quarther iv a dollar. Th' lad afoot invies th' dhriver, an' th' dhriver invies me; an' I might invy big Cleveland if it wasn't f'r th' hivinly smell iv this here noggin. An' who does Cleveland invy? Sure, it'd be sacreliege f'r me to say.

"Me ol' father, who was a full iv sayin's as an almanac, used to sink his spoon into th' stirabout, an' say, 'Well, lads, this ain' bacon an' greens an' porther; but it'll be annything ye like i ye'll on'y think iv th' Cassidys.' Th' Cassidys was th' poores fam'ly in th' parish. They waked th' oldest son in small beer an' was little thought of. Did me father iver ask thim in to share th' stirabout? Not him. An' he was the kindest man in th' wurruld He had a heart in him as big as a lump iv turf, but he'd say 'Whin ye grow up, take no wan's sorrows to ye'ersilf,' he says ''Tis th' wise man that goes through life thinkin' iv himsilf, fill his own stomach, an' takes away what he can't ate in his pocket. An' he was r-right, Jawn. We have throubles enough iv our own Th' wurruld goes on just th' same, an' ye can find fifty men t say th' lit'ny f'r ye to wan that'll give ye what'll relieve a fastin spit. Th' dead ar-re always pop'lar. I knowed a society wanst t vote a monyment to a man an' refuse to help his fam'ly, all i wan night. 'Tis cowld outside th' dure, ye say, but 'tis war-rum in here; an' I'm gettin' in me ol' age to think that the diff'renc between hivin an' hell is no broader"—

Mr. Dooley's remarks were cut short by a cry from the bacl room. It was unmistakably a baby's cry. Mr. McKenna turned suddenly in amazement as Mr. Dooley bolted.

"Well, in the name of the saints, what's all this?" he cried following his friend into the back room. He found the philos opher, with an expression of the utmost sternness, sitting on th side of his bed, with a little girl of two or three in his arms. Th philosopher was singing:—

> Ar-rah rock-a-bye, babby, on th' three top:
> Whin th' wind blo-ows, th' cradle ull r-rock;
> An', a-whin th' bough breaks, th' cradle ull fa-a-a-ll,
> An' a-down ull come babby, cradle, an' all.

Then he sang:—

> In th' town iv Kilkinny there du-wilt a fair ma-aid,
> In th' town iv Kilkinny there du-wilt a fair ma-aid.
> She had cheeks like th' roses, an' hair iv th' same,
> An' a mouth like ripe sthrawburries burrid in crame.

He rocked the child to and fro, and its crying ceased while he sang: —

> Chip, chip, a little horse;
> Chip, chip, again, sir.
> How manny miles to Dublin?
> Threescure an' tin, sir.

The little girl went to sleep on Mr. Dooley's white apron. He lifted her tenderly, and carried her over to his bed. Then he tiptoed out with an apprehensive face, and whispered: "It's Jawn Donahue's kid that wandherd away fr'm home, an' wint to sleep on me dure-step. I sint th' Dorsey boy to tell th' mother, but he's a long time gone. Do ye run over, Jawn, an' lave thim know."

On Nansen

"I SEE," said Mr. Dooley, "that Doc Nansen has come back."

"Yes," said Mr. McKenna. "It's a wonder he wouldn't stay till winter. If I was setting on an iceberg in latitude umpty-ump north of Evanston these days, they couldn't pry me off it with a crowbar. Not they."

"He had to come back," explained Mr. Hennessy. "He got as far as he cud, an' thin he was foorced be th' inclimincy iv th' weather to return to his home in Feechoold, Norway."

"To where?" Mr. Dooley asked contemptuously.

"To Foocheeld, Norway," said Mr. Hennessy, with some misgivings.

"Ye don't know what ye're talkin' about," retorted the philosopher. "Ye ought to go back to school an' study gee-ography. Th' place he come back to was Oostook, Norway, between Coopenhaagen an'—an' Rogers Park."

"Maybe ye're right," said Mr. Hennessy. "Annyhow, he come back, chased be a polar bear. It must iv been a thrillin' experience, leppin' fr'm iceberg to iceberg, with a polar bear grabbin' at th' seat iv his pants, an' now an' thin a walrus swoopin' down fr'm a three an' munchin' his hat."

"What ta-alk have ye?" Mr. Dooley demanded. "A walrus don't fly, foolish man!"

"What does he do, thin?" asked Mr. Hennessy. "Go 'round on crutches?"

"A walrus," said Mr. Dooley, "is an animal something like a hor-rse, but more like a balloon. It doesn't walk, swim, or fly. It rowls whin pur-suin' its prey. It whirls 'round an' 'round at a speed akel to a railroad injine, meltin' th' ice in a groove behind it. Tame walruses are used be th' Eskeemyoos, th' old settlers iv thim parts, as lawnmowers an' to press their clothes. Th' wild walrus is a mos' vicious animal, which feeds on snowballs through th' day, an' thin goes out iv nights afther artic explorers, which for-rms its principal diet. Theyse a gr-reat demand among walruses f'r artic explorers, Swedes preferred; an' on account iv th' scarcity iv this food it isn't more than wanst in twenty years that th' walrus gets a square meal. Thin he devours his victim, clothes, collar-buttons, an' all."

"Well, well," said Mr. Hennessy. "I had no idee they was that ferocious. I thought they were like bur-rds. Don't they lay eggs?"

"Don't they lay eggs?" Mr. Dooley replied. "Don't they lay eggs? Did ye iver hear th' like iv that, Jawn? Why, ye gaby, ye might as well ask me does a pianny lay eggs. Iv coorse not."

"I'd like to know what the objict of these here arctic explorations is," interposed Mr. McKenna, in the interests of peace.

"Th' principal objict is to get rid iv an over-supply iv foolish people," said Mr. Dooley. "In this counthry, whin a man begins f'r to see sthrange things, an' hitch up cockroaches, an' think he's Vanderbilt dhrivin' a four-in-hand, we sind him to what me ol' frind Sleepy Burk calls th' brain college. But in Norway an' Sweden they sind him to th' North Pole, an' feed him to th' polar bears an' th' walruses. A man that scorches on a bicycle or wears a pink shirt or is caught thryin' to fry out a stick iv dinnymite in a kitchen stove is given a boat an' sint off to play with Flora an' Fauna in th' frozen North."

"That's what I'd like to know," said Mr. Hennessy. "Who ar-re these Flora an' Fauna? I see be th' pa-aper that Doc Nansen stopped at Nootchinchoot Islands, an' saw Flora an' Fauna; an' thin, comin' back on th' ice, he encountherd thim again."

"I suppose," said Mr. Dooley, "ye think Flora an' Fauna is two little Eskeemy girls at skip-rope an' 'London bridge is fallin' down' on th' icebergs an' glaziers. It's a pretty idee ye have iv th' life in thim parts. Little Flora an' little Fauna playin' stooptag aroun' a whale or rushin' th' can f'r their poor tired father just home fr'm th' rollin'-mills, where he's been makin' snow-balls f'r th' export thrade, or engagin' in some other spoort iv childhood! Go wan with ye!"

"But who are they, annyhow?"

"I make it a rule in me life not to discuss anny woman's character," replied Mr. Dooley, sternly. "If Doc Nansen was off there skylarkin' with Flora an' Fauna, it's his own business, an' I make no inquiries. A lady's a lady, be she iver so humble; an', as Shakespeare says, cursed be th' man that'd raise an ax to her, save in th' way iv a joke. We'll talk no scandal in this house, Hinnissy."

But, after his friend had gone, Mr. Dooley leaned over confidentially, and whispered to Mr. McKenna, "But who are Flora an' Fauna, Jawn?"

"I don't know," said Mr. McKenna.

"It sounds mighty suspicious, annyhow," said the philosopher. "I hope th' doc'll be able to square it with his wife."

On a Populist Convention

"KEEP ye'er eye on th' Pops, Jawn. They're gr-reat people an' a gr-reat pa-arty. What is their principles? Anny ol' thing that th' other pa-arties has rijected. Some iv thim is in favor iv coining money out iv baled hay an' dhried apples at a ratio iv sixteen to wan, an' some is in favor iv coinin' on'y th' apples. Thim are th' inflationists. Others want th' gover'mint to divide up the rivinues equally among all la-ads that's too sthrong to wurruk. Th' Pops is again th' banks an' again the supreme court an again havin' gas that can be blowed out be th' human lungs. A sthrong section is devoted to th' principal iv separatin' Mark Hanna fr'm his money.

"A ma-an be th' name iv Cassidy, that thravels f'r a liquor-house, was in to see me this mornin'; an' he come fr'm Saint Looey. He said it beat all he iver see or heerd tell of. Whin th' con-vintion come to ordher, th' chairman says, 'La-ads, we'll open proceedin's be havin' th' Hon'rable Rube Spike, fr'm th' imperyal Territ'ry iv Okalahoma, cough up his famous song, "Pa-pa Cleveland's Teeth are filled with Goold."' 'Mr. Chairman,' says a delegate fr'm New Mexico, risin' an' wavin' his boots in th' air, 'if th' skate fr'm Okalahoma is allowed f'r to belch anny in this here assimblage, th' diligates fr'm th' imperyal Ter-rit'ry iv New Mexico'll lave th' hall. We have,' he says, 'in our mist th' Hon'rable Lafayette Hadley, whose notes,' he says, 'falls as sweetly on th' ear,' he says, 'as th' plunk iv hivin's rain in a

113

bar'l,' he says. 'If annywan has a hemorrhage iv anthems in this hall, it'll be Lafe Hadley, th' Guthrie batsoon,' he says. 'Ye shall not,' he says, 'press down upon our bleedin' brows,' he says, 'this cross iv thorns,' he says. 'Ye shall not crucify th' diligates fr'm th' imperyal Territ'ry iv New Mexico on this cross iv a Mississippi nigger an' Crow Injun fr'm Okalahoma,' he says. Thereupon, says me frind Cassidy, th' New Mexico diligation left th' hall, pursued be th' diligation from Oklahoma.

"Th' chairman knowed his business. 'In ordher,' he says, 'that there may be no disordher,' he says, 'I will call upon th' imperyal States,' he says, 'an' Territ'ries,' he says, 'beginnin' with th' imperyal State iv Alabama,' he says, 'to each sind wan singer to th' platform,' he says, 'f'r to wring out hear-rts with melodies,' he says. 'Meantime,' says he, 'pathrites who have diff'rences iv opinyon on anny questions can pro-cure ex-helves be applyin' to th' sergeant-at-arms,' he says. 'Now,' he says, 'if th' gintleman fr'm th' imperyal State of Mizzoury'll hand me up a cheek full iv his eatin' tobacco,' he says, 'we'll listen to Willyum G. Rannycaboo, th' boy melodjun iv th' imperyal State iv Alabama,' he says, 'who'll discoorse his well-known ballad, 'Th' Supreme Court is Full iv Standard Ile,' he says.

"Whin th' singin' had con-cluded, so me frind Cassidy says, th' chair announced that speakin' would be in ordher, an' th' con-vintion rose as wan man. Afther ordher had been enforced be th' sergeant-at-arms movin' round, an' lammin' diligates with a hoe, a tall man was seen standin' on a chair. F'r some moments th' chairman was onable to call his name, but he fin'lly found a place to spill; an' in a clear voice he says, 'F'r what purpose does th' gintleman fr'm the imperyal State iv Texas arise?' 'I arise,' says th' ma-an, 'f'r th' purpose iv warnin' this con-vintion that we have a goold-bug in our mist,' he says. Cries iv 'Throw him out!' 'Search him!' 'Hang him!' arose. 'In wandhrin' through th' hall, I just seen a man with a coat on,' he says. Great excitement ensood, says me frind Cassidy; an' th' thremblin' victim was brought down th' aisle. 'What have ye to say f'r ye'ersilf?' demands th' chairman in thundhrin' tones. 'On'y this,' says th' goold-bug. 'I wandhered in here, lookin' f'r frinds,' he says. 'I am not a goold-bug,' he says. 'I wear me coat,' he says, 'because I have no shirt,' he says. 'Gintlemen,' says th' chairman, 'a mistake

114

has been made,' he says. 'This here person, who bears th' appearance iv a plutocrat, is all right underneath,' he says. 'He's a diligate to th' silver convintion,' he says. 'Go in peace,' he says.

"Be this time 'twas gr-rowin' late, an' th' convintion adjourned. 'Befure ye lave,' says th' chairman, 'I have to announce that on account iv th' chairman of the comity havin' been imprisoned in a foldin'-bed an' th' sicrity havin' mistook th' fire extinguisher f'r a shower bath, they'll be no meetin' iv th' comity on rules till to-morrow night. Durin' th' interval,' he says, 'th' convintion'll continue ketch-as-ketch can,' he says."

"Well," said Mr. McKenna, "to think of taking this here country out of the hands of William C. Whitney and Grover Cleveland and J. Pierpont Morgan and Ickleheimer Thalmann, and putting it in the hands of such men. What do you think about it?"

"I think," said Mr. Dooley, "that Cassidy lied."

On a Family Reunion

"WHY aren't you out attending the reunion of the Dooley family?" Mr. McKenna asked the philosopher.

"Thim's no rel-ations to me," Mr. Dooley answered. "Thim's farmer Dooleys. No wan iv our fam'ly iver lived in th' counthry. We live in th' city, where they burn gas an' have a polis foorce to get on to. We're no farmers, divvle th' bit. We belong to th' industhreel classes. Thim must be th' Fermanagh Dooleys, a poor lot, Jawn, an' always on good terms with th' landlord, bad ciss to thim, says I. We're from Roscommon. They'se a Dooley family in Wixford an' wan near Ballybone that belonged to th' constabulary. I met him but wanst. 'Twas at an iviction; an', though he didn't know me, I inthrajooced mesilf be landin' him back iv th' ear with a bouldher th' size iv ye'er two fists together. He didn't know me aftherwards, ayether.

"We niver had but wan reunion iv th' Dooley fam'ly, an' that was tin years ago. Me cousin Felix's boy Aloysius,—him that aftherwards wint to New York an' got a good job dhrivin' a carredge f'r th' captain iv a polis station,—he was full iv pothry an' things; an' he come around wan night, an' says he, 'D'ye know,' he says, ''twud be th' hite iv a good thing f'r th' Dooleys to have a reunion,' he says. 'We ought to come together,' he says, 'an' show the people iv this ward,' he says, 'how sthrong we are,' he says. 'Ye might do it betther, me buck,' says I, 'shovellin' slag at th' mills,' I says. 'But annyhow, if ye'er mind's set on it, go

116

ahead,' I says, 'an' I'll attind to havin' th' polis there,' I says, 'f'r I have a dhrag at th' station.'

"Well, he sint out letthers to all th' Roscommon Dooleys; an' on a Saturdah night we come together in a rinted hall an' held th' reunion. 'Twas great sport f'r a while. Some iv us hadn't spoke frindly to each other f'r twinty years, an' we set around an' tol' stories iv Roscommon an' its green fields, an' th' stirabout pot that was niver filled, an' th' blue sky overhead an' th' boggy ground undherfoot. 'Which Dooley was it that hamsthrung th' cows?' 'Mike Dooley's Pat.' 'Naw such thing: 'twas Pat Dooley's Mike. I mane Pat Dooley's Mike's Pat.' F'r 'tis with us as with th' rest iv our people. Ye take th' Dutchman: he has as manny names to give to his childher as they'se nails in his boots, but an Irishman has th' pick iv on'y a few. I knowed a man be th' name iv Clancy,—a man fr'm Kildare. He had fifteen childher; an', whin th' las' come, he says, 'Dooley, d'ye happen to know anny saints?' 'None iv thim thrades here,' says I. 'Why?' says I. 'They'se a new kid at th' house,' he says; 'an', be me troth, I've run out iv all th' saints I knew, an', if somewan don't come to me assistance, I'll have to turn th' child out on th' wurruld without th' rag iv a name to his back,' he says.

"But I was tellin' ye about th' reunion. They was lashins iv dhrink an' story-tellin', an' Felix's boy Aloysius histed a banner he had made with 'Dooley aboo' painted on it. But, afther th' night got along, some iv us begun to raymimber that most iv us hadn't been frinds f'r long. Mrs. Morgan Dooley, she that was Molly Dooley befure she married Morgan, she turns to me, an' says she, "Tis sthrange they let in that Hogan woman,' she says,—that Hogan woman, Jawn, bein' th' wife iv her husband's brother. She heerd her say it, an' she says, 'I'd have ye to undherstand that no wan iver come out iv Roscommon that cud hold up their heads with th' Hogans,' she says. "Tis not f'r th' likes iv ye to slandher a fam'ly that's iv th' landed gintry iv Ireland, an' f'r two pins I'd hit ye a poke in th' eye,' she says. If it hadn't been f'r me bein' between thim, they'd have been trouble; f'r they was good frinds wanst. What is it th' good book says about a woman scorned? Faith, I've forgotten.

"Thin me uncle Mike come in, as rough a man as iver laid hands on a polisman. Felix Dooley was makin' a speech on th' vartues iv th' fam'ly. 'Th' Dooleys,' says he, 'can stand befure all th' wurruld, an' no man can say ought agin ayether their honor or their integrity,' says he. 'Th' man that's throwin' that at ye,' says me uncle Mike, 'stole a saw fr'm me in th' year sivinty-five.' Felix paid no attintion to me uncle Mike, but wint on, 'We point proudly to th' motto, "Dooley aboo—Dooley f'river." ' 'Th' saw aboo,' says uncle Mike. 'Th' Dooleys,' says Felix, 'stood beside Red Hugh O'Neill; an', whin he cut aff his hand,—' 'He didn't cut it off with anny wan else's saw,' says me uncle Mike. 'They'se an old sayin',' wint on Felix. 'An' ol' saw,' says me uncle Mike. 'But 'twas new whin ye stole it.'

" 'Now look here,' says Aloysius, 'this thing has gone far enough. 'Tis an outrage that this here man shud come here f'r to insult th' head iv th' fam'ly.' 'Th' head iv what fam'ly?' says Morgan Dooley, jumpin' up as hot as fire. 'I'm th' head iv th' fam'ly,' he says, 'be right iv histhry.' 'Ye're an ol' cow,' says me uncle Mike. 'Th' back iv me hand an' th' sowl iv me fut to all iv ye,' he says. 'I quit ye,' he says. 'Ye're all livin' here undher assumed names'; an' he wint out, followed be Morgan Dooley with a chair in each hand.

"Well, they wasn't two Dooleys in th' hall'd speak whin th' meetin' broke up; an' th' Lord knows, but I don't to this day, who's th' head iv th' Dooley fam'ly. All I know is that I had wan th' nex' mornin'."

On a Famous Wedding

"YE see, Jawn," he said, " 'twas this way: The Jook iv Marlburrow is a young lad an' poor. Ye can't think of a jook bein' poor, but 'tis a fact that they'se many a wan iv thim that's carryin' th' banner at this minyit. Hinnissy, if he had his rights, is Jook iv Munster; an' ye know what he's got. The Jook iv Marlburrow, whin he come out iv th' academy where they had him, he hadn't a cint to his name. Ne'er a wan.

"They ain't manny jobs f'r a young jook. Th' thrade is limited; an' this here la-ad wint round night an' day lookin' f'r a sign, 'Wanted, a young jook, r-ready an' willin' to do light family jookin'.' an' no sign did he see. He was in a bad way; f'r the la-ad's father was dead, th' ol' jook. He was a fine bucko. He had a divorce fr'm his wife, an' marrid another; an', whin he died, she marrid somewan else an' took the roly-boly with her. This was ha-ard on th' lad.

"But he come iv a noble race, an' wan that had reed burruds whin their betthers had snowballs. Did ye iver read histhry, Jawn? Ye ought to. 'Tis betther thin th' Polis Gazette, an' near as thrue. Well, Jawn, this here young man come fr'm a gr-reat gin'ral, a fine-lookin' la-ad that had manny a mash in his day, an' niver lost money be wan iv thim. Ye'll find all about him in Casey's 'Histhry iv English Misrule in Ireland: Th' Story iv a Crime.' 'Tis good readin'.

"Th' la-ad's father marrid a rich woman. So did his uncle. So

119

ye see he was a natural bor-rn fi-nanceer. An' he begun to luk around him f'r what th' pa-apers calls a 'financee.'

"He didn't have far to go. I dinnaw how he done it, whether th' Ganderbilks asked him 'r he asked th' Ganderbilks. Annyhow, 'twas arranged. 'Twas horse an' horse between thim. Th' Ganderbilks had money, an' he was a jook. They was wan divorce on each side. So they imported him over, what they call assisted immygration. He didn't come undher th' head iv skilled workman. They must've classed him as a domestic servant. Th' first thing he done was to get himsilf arristed. A man be th' name iv Sweeney, — there are some good Sweeneys, though it's a name I don't like on account iv wan iv thim stealin' me fa-ather's grin'stone, — a man be th' name iv Sweeney, a polisman, r-run him in f'r disordherly conduct. They got him out with a pull. Thin he sint f'r lawyers an' f'r his financee's father, an' they settled down to talk business. 'Well,' says Ganderbilk, 'how much d'ye want?' he says. 'I'll give ye a millyon.' 'Goowan,' says th' jook, 'I cud get that much marryin' somewan I knew.' 'Thin how much d'ye want?' says Ganderbilk. 'Well,' says th' jook, 'th' castle has to be put in repair. Th' plumbin' is all gone to th' divvle, an' they'll have to be a new catch-basin put in,' he says. 'Thin they'se calciminin' an' paper-hangin', — well, call it tin millyons.' 'But what do I get out iv it?' says Ganderbilk. 'Have ye a ticket to th' church to see me marrid?' says th' jook. 'No,' says his pappa-in-law. 'Well, here's a couple,' says th' jook. 'Bring wan iv ye'er frinds with ye.' So Ganderbilk he coughed.

They say th' jook was that poor he had to have his coat made out iv what was left over fr'm his pants, they do so. But he was at th' church bright an' early; an' Ganderbilk he was there, too, standin' out on th' steps in th' cold, combin' his whiskers — he wears a pair iv sluggers — with his fingers. Afther awhile his daughter, the jook's financee, come along; an', seein' the jook, says she, 'Pappa,' she says, 'inthrojooce me to ye'er frind.' 'Jook,' says Ganderbilk, 'shake hands with me daughther. She's your's,' he says. An' so they were marrid.

"Well, Jawn," said Mr. Dooley, becoming serious, " 'tis a dhroll wurruld, an' I suppose we've got to take th' jooks an' th' Ganderbilks with the r-rest. I'm goin' to a weddin' mesilf nex' week. Th' banns has been called between little Dalia Hogan an' big

Tom Moran. They've been engaged f'r three year, her wurrkin' in a box facthry an' him doin' overtime at th' blast. They've money enough to start, an' it'll not cost ol' ma-an Hogan a cint. But, whin he spoke about it las' night, he cried as if his heart'd break."

On a Quarrel between England and Germany

MR. MCKENNA was aware that a gentle feud had existed between Mr. Dooley and Mr. Schwartzmeister, the German saloon-keeper down Archey Road, for some years. It was based upon racial differences, but had been accented when Mr. Schwartzmeister put in a pool table. Of course there was no outburst. When the two met on the street, Mr. Dooley saluted his neighbor cordially, in these terms: "Good-nobben, Hair Schwartzmeister, an' vas magst too yet, me brave bucko!" To which Mr. Schwartzmeister invariably retorted: "Py chapers, Tooley, where you haf been all der time, py chapers?" But this was mere etiquette. In the publicity of their own taverns they entertained no great regard for each other. Mr. Schwartzmeister said a friend of his had been poisoned by Mr. Dooley's beer, and Mr. Dooley confessed that he would rather go to a harness-shop for whiskey than to Mr. Schwartzmeister's. Consequently, Mr. McKenna was amazed to learn that Mr. Schwartzmeister had been entertained by the philosopher, and that they had paraded Archey Road arm-in-arm at a late hour.

"Tubby sure he was," said Mr. Dooley.

"Tubby sure he was. Right where ye're standin' at this moment, me dhrinkin' beer an' him callin' f'r hot Irish. 'Make it hot,' he says. 'Make it hot, me frind; an' we'll make it hot f'r th' British between us,' says Schwartzmeister.

"It come about this way: Ye see Willum Joyce come in, an'

says he, 'We've got thim.' 'Sure,' says I. 'We've the comityman, haven't we?' 'Th' Dutch is with us,' he says. 'I mane the Germans is our frinds.' 'Ye're goin' too far there,' says I. 'Stuckart was again Reed las' spring.' 'No, no,' says Willum Joyce, he says. 'Th' Germans is up in ar-rms again th' Sassenach,' he says, ''tis our jooty to be frindly with th' Germans,' he says. 'I'm now on me way f'r to organ-ize a camp iv me Dutch frinds down be th' slough,' he says. An' off he goes.

" 'Twas not long afther whin I heerd a man singin' 'Th' Wearin' iv th' Green' down th' sthreet, an' in come Schwartz-meister. 'Faugh a ballagh,' says he, meanin' to be polite. 'Lieb vaterland,' says I. An' we had a dhrink together.

" 'Vell,' says he (ye know th' murdhrin' way he has iv speakin'), 'here we are,' he says, 'frinds at las'.' 'Thrue f'r ye,' says I. 'Tooley,' he says, f'r he calls me that, 'we're wan to-night, alretty,' he says. 'We are that,' says I. 'But, glory be, who iver thought th' Irish'd live to see th' day whin they'd be freed be th' Dutch? Schwartz, me lieber frind,' I says, 'here's a health to th' imp'ror, hock,' says I. 'Slanthu,' says he; an' we had wan.

" ' 'Twud be a great combination,' says I. 'We'd carry th' wa-ard be th' biggest majority iver heerd iv,' I says. 'We wud so,' says he. 'I'd be aldherman.' 'Afther me,' says I. ''Tis my turn first,' I says. 'I don't know about that,' says he. 'Now,' says I, 'look here, Schwartzmeister,' I says. 'This here arrangement be-tween Germany an' Ireland has got to be brought down to th' Sixth Wa-ard,' I says. 'Do ye f'rgive th' way we done ye in th' beer rites?' I says. 'I do,' says he. 'They was befure me time.' 'Well,' says I, 'are ye sure ye can get over th' whalin' ye got whin th' Sarsfield Fife an' Dhrum Corpse met th' Frederick Willum Picnic Band?' I says. 'I do,' says he. 'An' ye have no har-rd feelin' about th' way th' bridges has been give out?' 'Not a thrace,' says he. 'Well,' says I, 'Schwartz,' I says, 'they'se wan thing more,' I says. 'We're both pathrites,' I says. 'We have a common cause,' I says. 'Ye're a Dutchman, an' I'm iv th' other sort,' I says. 'But we're both again th' Sassenach,' I says. 'An' in th' inthrests iv th' freedom iv Ireland,' I says, 'I f'rgive ye th' pool table.'

"Well, sir, Jawn, he wept like a child. 'Tooley,' he says, 'we'll march side be side,' he says. 'Both iv us in th' front rank,' he says. 'Aldherman Tooley an' Aldherman Schwartzmeister, to free

123

Ireland,' he says. 'But where does Germany come in?' he says. 'Germany!' says I, 'Germany! Well, we'll take care iv Germany, all right. We'll let Germans into th' prim'ries,' I says. An' there an' thin we formed th' Sarsfield-an'-Gatty camp. Gatty is a German frind iv Schwartzmeister. We shook dice to see which name'd come first. Ireland won. They was my dice.

"I learned Schwartzmeister th' Shan-van-Voght befure we was through; an' I've got th' German naytional chune be heart, — 'Ich vice nit wauss allus bay doitan.' What'll ye have to drink, Jawn?"

And, as Mr. McKenna went out, he heard his friend muttering: "Freed be th' Dutch! Freed be the Dutch! An' we niver give thim so much as a dillygate."

On Oratory in Politics

"I MIND th' first time Willum J. O'Brien r-run f'r office, th' Raypublicans an' th' Indypindants an' th' Socialists an' th' Prohybitionist (he's dead now, his name was Larkin) nommynated a young man be th' name iv Dorgan that was in th' law business in Halsted Sthreet, near Cologne, to r-run again' him. Smith O'Brien Dorgan was his name, an' he was wan iv th' most iloquint young la-ads that iver made a speakin' thrumpet iv his face. He cud holler like th' impire iv a base-ball game; an', whin he delivered th' sintimints iv his hear-rt, ye'd think he was thryin' to confide thim to a man on top iv a high buildin'. He was prisidint iv th' lithry club at th' church; an' Father Kelly tol' me that, th' day afther he won th' debate on th' pen an' th' soord in favor iv th' pen, they had to hire a carpenter to mend th' windows, they'd sagged so. They called him th' boy or-rator iv Healey's slough.

"He planned th' campaign himsilf. 'I'll not re-sort,' says he, 'to th' ordin'ry methods,' he says. 'Th' thing to do,' he says, 'is to prisint th' issues iv th' day to th' voters,' he says. 'I'll burn up ivry precin't in th' ward with me iloquince,' he says. An' he brought a long black coat, an' wint out to spread th' light.

"He talked ivrywhere. Th' people jammed Finucane's Hall, an' he tol' thim th' time had come f'r th' masses to r-rise. 'Raymimber,' says he, 'th' idees iv Novimb'r,' he says. 'Raymimber Demosthens an' Cicero an' Oak Park,' he says. 'Raymimber th'

125

thraditions iv ye'er fathers, iv Washin'ton an' Jefferson an' An-
dhrew Jackson an' John L. Sullivan,' he says. 'Ye shall not, Billy
O'Brien,' he says, 'crucify th' voters iv th' Sixth Ward on th'
double cross,' he says. He spoke to a meetin' in Deerin' Sthreet
in th' same wuruds. He had th' sthreet-car stopped while he
coughed up reemarks about th' Constitution until th' bar-rn boss
sint down an' threatened to discharge Mike Dwyer that was
dhrivin' wan hundherd an' eight in thim days, though thrans-
ferred to Wintworth Avnoo later on. He made speeches to polismin in th' squadroom an' to good la-ads hoistin' mud out iv
th' dhraw at th' red bridge. People'd be settin' quite in th' back
room playin' forty-fives whin Smith O'Brien Dorgan'd burst in,
an' addhress thim on th' issues iv th' day.

"Now all this time Bill O'Brien was campaignin' in his own
way. He niver med wan speech. No wan knew whether he was
f'r a tariff or again wan, or whether he sthud be Jefferson or
was knockin' him, or whether he had th' inthrests iv th' toilin'
masses at hear-rt or whether he wint to mass at all, at all. But
he got th' superintindint iv th' rollin'-mills with him; an' he put
three or four good faml'ies to wurruk in th' gas-house, where
he knew th' main guy, an' he made reg'lar calls on th' bar-rn
boss iv th' sthreet-ca-ars. He wint to th' picnics, an' hired th' orchesthry f'r th' dances, an' voted himsilf th' most pop'lar man
at th' church fair at an expinse iv at laste five hundherd dollars.
No wan that come near him wanted f'r money. He had head-
quarthers in ivry saloon fr'm wan end iv th' ward to th' other.
All th' pa-apers printed his pitcher, an' sthud by him as th' frind
iv th' poor.

"Well, people liked to hear Dorgan at first, but afther a few
months they got onaisy. He had a way iv breakin' into festive
gatherin's that was enough to thry a saint. He delayed wan prize
fight two hours, encouragin' th' voters prisint to stand be their
principles, while th' principles sat shiverin' in their cor-rners
until th' polis r-run him out. It got so that men'd bound into
alleys whin he come up th' sthreet. People in th' liquor business
rayfused to let him come into their places. His fam'ly et in th'
coal-shed f'r fear iv his speeches at supper. He wint on talkin',
and Willum J. O'Brien wint on handin' out th' dough that he
got fr'm th' gas company an' con-ciliatin' th' masses; an', whin

126

iliction day come, th' judges an' clerks was all f'r O'Brien, an' Dorgan didn't get votes enough to wad a gun. He sat up near all night in his long coat, makin' speeches to himsilf; but tord mornin' he come over to my place where O'Brien sat with his la-ads. 'Well,' says O'Brien, 'how does it suit ye?' he says. 'It's sthrange,' says Dorgan. 'Not sthrange at all,' says Willum J. O'Brien. 'Whin ye've been in politics as long as I have, ye'll know,' he says, 'that th' roly-boly is th' gr-reatest or-rator on earth,' he says. 'Th' American nation in th' Sixth Ward is a fine people,' he says. 'They love th' eagle,' he says, 'on th' back iv a dollar,' he says. 'Well,' says Dorgan, 'I can't undherstand it,' he says. 'I med as manny as three thousan' speeches,' he says. 'Well,' says Willum J. O'Brien, 'that was my majority,' he says. 'Have a dhrink,' he says."

On Christmas Gifts

THE approach of Christmas is heralded in Archey Road by many
of the signs that are known to the less civilized and more prosperous parts of the city. The people look poorer, colder, and
more hopeful than at other times. The bakeries assume an old
country appearance of gayety. The saloons are well filled. Also,
if you have your eyes about you, you may catch a glimpse, now
and then, through a frosted window-pane of a stunted Christmas
tree, laden slenderly with glass balls and ropes of red popcorn,
the work of painful hands after the childher are abed. Mr. Dooley
knew Christmas was coming by the calendar, the expiration of
his quarterly license, and Mr. Hennessy coming in with a doll
in his pocket and a rockingchair under his arm.

"Prisints?" said the philosopher.

"Yis," said Mr. Hennessy. "I had to do it. I med up me mind
this year that I wudden't buy anny Chris'mas prisints or take
anny. I can't afford it. Times has been fearful ha-ard, an' a look
iv pain comes over th' ol' woman's face whin I hold out fifty
cints fr'm me salary on Saturdah night. I give it out that I didn't
want annything, but they'se so much scurryin' ar-round an' hidin'
things whin I go in that I know they've got something f'r me.
I cudden't stand it no longer, so I wint down town tonight, down
be Shekel an' Whooper's place, an' bought these things. This is
a fine doll f'r th' money."

"It is," said Mr. Dooley, taking the doll and examining it with the eye of an art critic. "It closes its eyes, — yis, an', bedad, it cries if ye punch it. They're makin' these things more like human bein's ivry year. An' does it say pap-pah an' mam-mah, I dinnaw?"

"No," said Mr. Hennessy, "th' pap-pah an' mam-mah dolls costs too much."

"Well," continued Mr. Dooley, "we can't have ivrything we want in this wurruld. If I had me way, I'd buy goold watches an' chains f'r ivrybody in th' r-road, an' a few iv th' good Germans. I feel that gin'rous. But 'tis no use. Ye can't give what ye want. Ivry little boy ixpects a pony at Chris'mas, an' ivry little girl a chain an' locket; an' ivry man thinks he's sure goin' to get th' goold-headed cane he's longed f'r since he come over. But they all fin'lly land on rockin'-horses an' dolls, an' suspindhers that r-run pink flowers into their shirts an' tattoo thim in summer. An' they conceal their grief Chris'mas mornin' an' thry to look pleasant with murdher in their hearts.

"Some wan has always give me a Chris'mas prisint, though no wan has anny r-right to. But no wan iver give me annything I cud wear or ate or dhrink or smoke or curl me hair with. I've had flasks iv whisky give me, — me that have lashin's iv whisky at me elbow day an' night; an', whin I opined thim, blue an' yellow flames come out an' some iv th' stuff r-run over on th' flure, an' set fire to th' buildin'. I smoke th' best five-cint seegar that money can buy; yet, whin a good frind iv mine wants to make me a prisint f'r Chris'mas, he goes to a harness shop an' buys a box iv see-gars with excelsior fillin's an' burlap wrappers, an', if I smoked wan an' lived, I'd be arristed f'r arson. I got a pair iv suspinders wanst fr'm a lady, — niver mind her name, — an' I wurruked hard that day; an' th' decorations moved back into me, an' I had to take thim out with pumice stone. I didn't lose th' taste iv th' paint f'r weeks an' weeks.

"Wan year I wanted a watch more thin annything in th' wurruld. I talked watches to ivry wan that I thought had designs on me. I made it a pint to ask me frinds what time iv night it was, an' thin say, 'Dear me, ought to get a watch if I cud affoord it.' I used to tout people down to th' jooler's shop, an' stand be th' window with a hungry look in th' eyes iv me, as much as to say, 'If I don't get a watch, I'll perish.' I talked watches an' thought watches an' dhreamed watches. Father Kelly rebuked me f'r bein' late f'r mass. 'How can I get there befure th' gospil, whin I don't know what time it is?' says I. 'Why don't ye luk at ye'er watch?' he says. 'I haven't none,' says I. Did he give me a watch? Faith, he did not. He sint me a box iv soap that made me smell like a coon goin' to a ball in a State Sthreet ca-ar. I got a necktie fr'm wan man; an', if I wore it to a meetin' iv th' Young Hebrews' Char'table Society, they'd've thrun me out. That man wanted me to be kilt. Another la-ad sint me a silk handkerchief that broke on me poor nose. Th' nearest I got to a watch was a hair chain that unravelled, an' made me look as if I'd been curryin' a Shetland pony. I niver got what I wanted, an I niver expect to. No wan does."

"I'll get ye what ye want," said Mr. Hennessy, "if ye'll tell me what it is, an' it don't cost too much."

"Will ye?" said Mr. Dooley, eagerly.

"I will," said Mr. Hennessy, "if 'tis within me means."

"Ye're jokin'," said Mr. Dooley.

"I'm not. I mane it."

"Do ye, honest?"

"I do so."

"Thin," said Mr. Dooley, "get me th' Audjitooroom. "I've wanted that to play with f'r manny years."

And Mr. Hennessy went away with the rocking-chair under his arm, the doll in his pocket, and dumb anger in his heart.

On Anarchists

" 'TIS ha-ard bein' a king these days," said Mr. Dooley. "Manny's th' man on a throne wishes his father'd brought him up a cooper, what with wages bein' docked be parlymints an' ragin' arnychists r-runnin' wild with dinnymite bombs undher their ar-rms an' carvin'-knives in their pockets.

"Onaisy, as Hogan says, is th' head that wears a crown. They'se other heads that're onaisy, too; but ye don't hear iv thim. But a man gr-ows up in wan iv thim furrin' counthries, an' he's thrained f'r to be a king. Hivin may've intinded him f'r a dooce or a jack, at th' most; but he has to follow th' same line as his father. 'Tis like pawn-brokin' that way. Ye niver heerd iv a pawn-broker's son doin' annything else. Wanst a king, always a king. Other men's sons may pack away a shirt in a thrunk, an' go out into th' wurruld, brakin' on a freight or ladin' Indyanny bankers up to a shell game. But a man that's headed f'r a throne can't r-run away. He's got to take th' job. If he kicks, they blindfold him an' back him in. He can't ask f'r his time at th' end iv th' week, an' lave. He pays himsilf. He can't sthrike, because he'd have to ordher out th' polis to subjoo himsilf. He can't go to th' boss, an' say: 'Me hours is too long an' th' wurruk is tajious. Give me me pay-check.' He has no boss. A man can't be indi-pindint onless he has a boss. 'Tis thrue. So he takes th' place, an' th' chances ar-re he's th' biggest omadhon in th' wurruld, an' knows no more about r-runnin' a counthry thin I know about

131

ladin' an orchesthry. An', if he don't do annything, he's a dummy, an', if he does do annything, he's crazy; an', whin he dies, his foreman says: 'Sure, 'tis th' divvle's own time I had savin' that bosthoon fr'm desthroyin' himsilf. If it wasn't f'r me, th' poor thing'd have closed down the wurruks, an' gone to th' far-rm long ago.' An' wan day, whin he's takin' th' air, p'raps, along comes an Eyetalyan, an' says he, 'Ar-re ye a king?' 'That's my name,' says his majesty. 'Betther dead,' says th' Eyetalyan; an' they'se a scramble, an' another king goes over th' long r-road.

"I don't know much about arnychists. We had thim here— wanst. They wint again polismen, mostly. Mebbe that's because polismen's th' nearest things to kings they cud find. But, an-nyhow, I sometimes think I know why they're arnychists some-where, an' why they ain't in other places. It minds me iv what happened wanst in me cousin Terence's fam'ly. They was livin' down near Healey's slough in wan iv thim ol' Doherty's houses,— not Doherty that ye know, th' j'iner, a good man whin he don't dhrink. No, 'twas an ol' grouch iv a man be th' name iv Malachi Doherty that used to keep five-day notices in his thrunk, an' ownded his own privit justice iv th' peace. Me cousin Terence was as dacint a man as iver shoed a hor-rse; an his wife was a good woman, too, though I niver took much to th' Dolans. Fr'm Tipperary, they was, an' too handy throwin' things at ye. An' he had a nice fam'ly growin' up, an' I niver knowed people that lived together more quite an' amyable. 'Twas good f'r to see thim settin' ar-roun' th' parlor,— Terence spellin' out th' news-paper, an' his good woman mendin' socks, an' Honoria playin' th' 'Vale iv Avoca' on th' pianny, an' th' kids r-rowlin' on th' flure.

"But wan day it happened that that whole fam'ly begun to rasp on wan another. Honoria'd set down at th' pianny, an' th' ol' man'd growl: 'F'r th' love iv th' saints, close down that hurdy-gurdy, an' lave a man injye his headache!' An' th' good woman scolded Terence, an' th' kids pulled th' leg fr'm undher th' stove; an', whin th' big boy Mike come home fr'm Omaha, he found none iv thim speakin' to th' others. He cud do nawthin', an' he wint f'r Father Kelly. Father Kelly sniffed th' air whin he come in; an' says he, 'Terence, what's th' matther with ye'er catch basin?' 'I dinnaw,' growled Terence. 'Well,' says Father Kelly, 'ye put on ye'er hat this minyit, an' go out f'r a plumber,' he says. 'I'm not needed here,' he says. 'Ye'er sowls ar-re all r-right,' he says; 'but ye'er systems ar-re out iv ordher,' he says. 'Fetch in a plumber,' he says, 'whilst I goes down to Doherty, an' make him think his lease on th' hereafther is defective,' he says."

"Ye're right," said Mr. Hennessy, who had followed the argument dimly.

"Iv coorse I'm right," said Mr. Dooley. "What they need over there in furrin' counthries is not a priest, but a plumber. 'Tis no good prayin' again arnychists, Hinnissy. Arnychists is sewer gas."

On the Dreyfus Case

"I SEE be th' pa-apers," said Mr. Dooley, "that Col. Hinnery, th' man that sint me frind Cap. Dhry-fuss to th' cage, has moved on. I sup-pose they'll give th' Cap a new thrile now."

"I hope they won't," said Mr. Hennessy. "I don't know an-nything about it, but I think he's guilty. He's a Jew."

"Well," said Mr. Dooley, "ye'er thoughts on this subject is inthrestin', but not conclusive, as Dorsey said to th' Pollack that thought he cud lick him. Ye have a r-right to ye'er opinyon, an' ye'll hold it annyhow, whether ye have a r-right to it or not. Like most iv ye'er fellow-citizens, ye start impartial. Ye don't know annything about th' case. If ye knew annything, ye'd not have an opinyon wan way or th' other. They'se niver been a matther come up in my time that th' American people was so sure about as they ar-re about th' Dhryfuss case. Th' Frinch ar-re not so sure, but they'se not a polisman in this counthry that can't tell ye jus' where Dhry-fuss was whin th' remains iv th' poor girl was found. That's because th' thrile was secret. If 'twas an open thrile, an' ye heerd th' tisti-mony, an' knew th' language, an' saw th' safe afther 'twas blown open, ye'd be puzzled, an' not care a rush whether Dhry-fuss was naked in a cage or takin' tay with his uncle at th' Benny Brith Club.

"I haven't made up me mind whether th' Cap done th' shootin' or not. He was certainly in th' neighborhood whin th' fire started, an' th' polis dug up quite a lot iv lead pipe in his back yard. But it's wan thing to sus-pect a man iv doin' a job an' another thing to prove that he didn't. Me frind Zola thinks he's innocint, an' he raised th' divvle at th' thrile. Whin th' judge come up on th' bench an' opined th' coort, Zola was settin' down below with th' lawyers. 'Let us pro-ceed,' says th' impartial an' fair-minded judge, 'to th' thrile iv th' haynious monsther Cap Dhry-fuss,' he says. Up jumps Zola, an' says he in Frinch: 'Jackuse,' he says, which is a hell of a mane thing to say to anny man. An' they thrun him out. 'Judge,' says th' attorney f'r th' difinse, 'an' gintlemen iv th' jury,' he says. 'Ye're a liar,' says th' judge. 'Cap, ye're guilty, an' ye know it,' he says. 'Th' decision iv th' coort is that ye be put in a cage, an' sint to th' Divvle's own island f'r th' r-rest iv ye'er life,' he says. 'Let us pro-ceed to hearin' th' tisti-mony,' he says. 'Call all th' witnesses at wanst,' he says, 'an' lave thim have it out on th' flure,' he says. Be this time Zola has come back; an' he jumps up, an', says he, 'Jackuse,' he says. An' they thrun him out.

"Befure we go anny farther,' says th' lawyer f'r th' difinse, 'I wish to sarve notice that, whin this thrile is over, I intind,' he says, 'to wait outside,' he says, 'an' hammer th' hon'rable coort into an omelet,' he says. 'With these few remarks I will close,' he says. 'Th' coort,' says th' judge, 'is always r-ready to defind th' honor iv France,' he says; 'an', if th' larned counsel will con-sint,' he says, 'to step up here f'r a minyit,' he says, 'th' coort'll put a sthrangle hold on him that'll not do him a bit iv good,' he says. 'Ah!' he says. 'Here's me ol' frind Pat th' Clam,' he says. 'Pat, what d'ye know about this case?' he says. 'Nine iv ye'er business,' says Pat. 'Answered like a man an' a sojer,' says th' coort. 'Jackuse,' says Zola fr'm th' dureway. An' they thrun him out. 'Call Col. Hinnery,' says th' coort. 'He ray-fuses to answer.' 'Good. Th' case is clear. Cap forged th' will. Th' coort will now adjourn f'r dools, an' all ladin' officers iv th' ar-rmy not in disgrace already will assimble in jail, an' com-mit suicide,' he says. 'Jackuse,' says Zola, an' started f'r th' woods, pursued be his fellow-editors. He's off somewhere in a three now hollerin' 'Jackuse' at ivry wan that passes, sufferin' martyrdom f'r his counthry an' writin' now an' thin about it all.

135

"That's all I know about Cap Dhry-fuss' case, an' that's all anny man knows. Ye didn't know as much, Hinnissy, till I told ye. I don't know whether Cap stole th' dog or not."

"What's he charged with?" Mr. Hennessy asked, in bewilderment.

"I'll niver tell ye," said Mr. Dooley. "It's too much to ask."

"Well, annyhow," said Mr. Hennessy, "he's guilty, ye can bet on that."

On the Decadence of Greece

"THAT young Hogan is a smart la-ad," said Mr. Dooley. "A smart la-ad an' a good wan, too."

"None betther," said Mr. Hennessy.

"None betther in th' ward," said Mr. Dooley, which was a high appreciation. "But there ar-re things about human nature an' histhry that ain't taught at Saint Ignateeus'. I tell thim to Hogan's la-ad.

"He was walkin' be th' store wan day las' week, an' I ast him how th' wa-ar wint. 'Tis sthrange, with churches two in a block, an' public schools as thick as lamp-posts, that, whin a man stops ye on th' sthreet, he'll ayether ast ye th' scoor iv th' base-ball game or talk iv th' Greek war with ye. I ain't seen annything that happened since Parnell's day that's aroused so much enthusyasm on th' Ar-rchey Road as th' Greek war. 'How goes th' war?' says I to young Hogan. 'How goes the war between th' ac-cursed infidel an' th' dog iv a Christian?' I says. 'It goes bad,' he says. 'Th' Greeks won a thremenjous battle, killin' manny millions iv th' Moslem murdherers, but was obliged to retreat thirty-two miles in a gallop,' 'Is that so?' says I. 'Sure that seems to be their luck,' I says. 'Whiniver they win, they lose; an', whin they lose, they lose,' I says. 'What ails thim?' I says. 'Is th' riferee again thim?' 'I can't make it out,' he says, while a tear sthud in his eye. 'Whin I think iv Leonidas at th' pass iv Thermometer,' he says, 'an' So-an'-so on th' field iv Marathon an' This-or-that

137

th' Spartan hero,' he says, 'I cannot undherstand f'r th' life iv me why th' Greeks shud have been dhruv fr'm pillar to post be an ar-rmy iv slaves. Didn't Leonidas, with hardly as manny men as there are Raypublicans in this precinct, hold th' pass again a savage horde?' he says. 'He did,' says I. 'He did.' 'An' didn't What's-his-name on th' field iv Marathon overcome an' desthroy th' ravagin' armies iv Persia?' he says. 'Thrue f'r ye,' says I. 'There's no doubt in th' wurruld about it,' I says. 'An' look at Alexander th' Great,' he says. 'Aleck was a turror, an' no mistake,' says I. 'An' Miltiades,' he says. 'I on'y know what I hear iv him,' says I. 'But fr'm all accounts he must have been consid'rable iv a fellow,' says I. 'An' in later days Marco Boozaris,' he says. 'He was th' man that come in con-sumption's dreaded form,' says I, 'an' he was afraid iv no man.' 'Well, thin,' says he, 'how ar-re we to account f'r this disgrace?' he says.

" 'Well,' says I, 'd'ye raymimber th' fightin' tenth precinct? Ye must've heerd ye'er father tell about it. It was famous f'r th' quality an' quantity iv th' warfare put up in it. Ivry man in th' tenth precinct cud fight his weight in scrap-iron. Most iv thim come fr'm th' ancient Hellenic province iv May-o; but they was a fair sprinklin' iv Greek heroes fr'm Roscommon an' Tipperary, an' a few from th' historic spot where th' Head iv Kinsale looks out on th' sea, an' th' sea looks up at th' Head iv Kinsale. Th' little boys cud box befure they was out iv skirts. Far an' wide, th' tenth precinct was th' turror iv its inimies. Ye talk about Leonidas an' th' pass iv Thermometer. Ye ought to've seen Mike Riordan an' his fam'ly defindin' th' pollin'-place whin Eddie Burke's brigade charged it wan fine day. That hero sthud f'r four hours in th' dureway, ar-rmed on'y with a monkey-wrinch, an' built a wall iv invaders in frint iv him till th' judges cud dig their way out through th' cellar, an' escape to th' polis station.

" 'F'r manny years th' tenth precinct was th' banner precinct iv th' Sixth Wa-ard, an' its gallant heroes repelled all attacks by land or Healey's slough. But, as time wint by, changes come over it. Th' Hannigans an' Leonidases an' Caseys moved out, havin' made their pile. Some iv th' grandest iv th' heroes died, an' their fam'lies were broke up. Polish Jews an' Swedes an' Germans an' Hollanders swarmed in, settlin' down on th' sacred sites,' I says. 'Wan night three years ago, a band iv rovin' Bohemians fr'm th'

Eighth Ward come acrost th' river, kickin' over bar'ls an' ash-boxes, an' swooped down on th' tenth precint. Mike Riordan, him that kept th' pollin'-place in th' good days iv old, was th' on'y wan iv th' race iv ancient heroes on earth. He thried to rally th' ingloryous descindants iv a proud people. F'r a while they made a stand in Halsted Sthreet, an' shouted bad but difficult names at th' infidel hordes, an' threw bricks that laid out their own people. But it was on'y f'r a moment. In another they tur-rned an' r-run, lavin' Mike Riordan standin' alone in th' mist iv th' fray. If it wasn't f'r th' intervintion iv th' powers in th' shape iv th' loot an' a wagon-load iv polismin, th' Bohemians'd have devastated as far as th' ruins iv th' gas-house, which is th' same as that there Acropulist ye talk about,' says I.

" 'No, my son,' says I. 'On account iv th' fluctuations in rint an' throuble with th' landlord it's not safe to presoom that th' same fam'ly always lives in th' wan house. Th' very thing happened to Greece that has happened to th' tenth precint iv th' Sixth Ward. Th' Greeks have moved out, an' th' Swedes come in. Ye yet may live to see th' day,' says I, 'whin what is thrue iv Athens an' th' tenth precint will be thrue iv th' whole Sixth Waard.' "

"Ye don't mean that," said Mr. Hennessy, gasping.

"I do," said Mr. Dooley, with solemnity. " 'Tis histhry."

On the Indian War

"GIN'RAL SHERMAN was wan iv th' smartest men iver had," said Mr. Dooley. "He said so manny bright things. 'Twas him said, 'War is hell'; an' that's wan iv th' finest sayin's I know annything about. 'War is hell': 'tis a thrue wurrud an' a fine sintiment. An' Gin'ral Sherman says, 'Th' on'y good Indyun is a dead Indyun.' An' that's a good sayin', too. So, be th' powers, we've started in again to improve th' race; an', if we can get in Gatlin' guns enough befure th' winter's snows, we'll tur-rn thim Chippeways into a cimitry branch iv th' Young Men's Christyan Association. We will so.

"Ye see, Hinnissy, th' Indyun is bound f'r to give way to th' onward march iv white civilization. You an' me, Hinnissy, is th' white civilization. I come along, an' I find ol' Snakes-in-his-Gaiters livin' quite an' dacint in a new frame house. Thinks I, ''Tis a shame f'r to lave this savage man in possession iv this fine abode, an' him not able f'r to vote an' without a frind on th' polis foorce.' So says I: 'Snakes,' I says, 'get along,' says I. 'I want ye'er house, an' ye best move out west iv th' thracks, an' dig a hole f'r ye'ersilf,' I says. 'Divvle th' fut I will step out iv this house,' says Snakes. 'I built it, an' I have th' law on me side,' he says. 'F'r why should I take Mary Ann, an' Terence, an' Honoria, an' Robert Immitt Snakes, an' all me little Snakeses, an' rustle out west iv th' thracks,' he says, 'far fr'm th' bones iv me ancestors,' he says, 'an beyond th' water-pipe extinsion,' he says. 'Because,' says I, 'I am th' walkin' dilygate iv white civilization,' I says. 'I'm jus' as civilized as you,' says Snakes. 'I wear pants,' he says, 'an' a plug hat,' he says. 'Ye might wear tin pair,' says I, 'an' all at wanst,' I says, 'an' ye'd still be a savage,' says I; 'an' I'd be civilized,' I says, 'if I hadn't on so much as a bangle bracelet,' I says. 'So get out,' says I. 'So get out,' says I, 'f'r th' pianny movers is outside, r-ready to go to wurruk,' I says.

"Well, Snakes he fires a stove lid at me; an' I go down to th' polis station, an' says I, 'Loot,' I says, 'they'se a dhrunken Indyun not votin' up near th' mills, an he's carryin' on outrageous, an' he won't let me hang me pitchers on his wall,' says I. 'Vile savage,' says th' loot, 'I'll tache him to rayspict th' rules iv civilization,' he says. An' he takes out a wagon load, an' goes afther Snakes. Well, me frind Snakes gives him battle, an', knowin' th' premises well, he's able to put up a gr-reat fight; but afther a while they rip him away, an' have him in th' pathrol wagon, with a man settin' on his head. An' thin he's put undher bonds to keep the peace, an' they sind him out west iv th' thracks; an' I move into th' house, an' tear out th' front an' start a faro bank. Some day, whin I get tired or th' Swedes dhrive me out or Schwartzmeister makes his lunch too sthrong f'r competition, I'll go afther Snakes again.

"Th' on'y hope f'r th Indyun is to put his house on rollers, an' keep a team hitched to it, an', whin he sees a white man, to start f'r th' settin' sun. He's rooned whin he has a cellar. He ought to put all th' plugged dollars that he gets from th' agent an' be pickin' blueberries into rowlin' stock. If he knew annything about balloons, he'd have a chanst; but we white men, Hinnissy, has all th' balloons. But, annyhow, he's doomed, as Hogan says. Th' onward march iv th' white civilization, with morgedges an' other modhern improvements, is slowly but surely, as Hogan says, chasin' him out; an' th' last iv him'll be livin' in a divin'-bell somewhere out in th' Pac-ific Ocean."

"Well," said Mr. Hennessy, the stout philanthropist, "I think so, an' thin again I dinnaw. I don't think we threat thim r-right. If I was th' gover'mint, I'd take what they got, but I'd say, 'Here, take this tin-dollar bill an' go out an' dhrink ye'ersilf to death,' I'd say. They ought to have some show."

"Well," said Mr. Dooley, "if ye feel that way, ye ought to go an' inlist as an Indyun."

On Golf

"AN' what's this game iv goluf like, I dinnaw?" said Mr. Hennessy, lighting his pipe with much unnecessary noise. "Ye're a good deal iv a spoort, Jawnny: did ye iver thry it?"

"No," said Mr. McKenna. "I used to roll a hoop onct upon a time, but I'm out of condition now."

"It ain't like base-ball," said Mr. Hennessy, "an' it ain't like shinny, an' it ain't like lawn-teenis, an' it ain't like forty-fives, an' it ain't"—

"Like canvas-back duck or anny other game ye know," said Mr. Dooley.

"Thin what is it like?" said Mr. Hennessy. "I see be th' pa-aper that Hobart What-d'ye-call-him is wan iv th' best at it. Th' other day he made a scoor iv wan hundherd an' sixty-eight, but whether 'twas miles or stitches I cudden't make out fr'm th' raypoorts."

" 'Tis little ye know," said Mr. Dooley. "Th' game iv goluf is as old as th' hills. Me father had goluf links all over his place, an', whin I was a kid, 'twas wan iv th' principal spoorts iv me life, afther I'd dug the turf f'r th' avenin', to go out and putt"—

"Poot, ye mean," said Mr. Hennessy. "They'se no such wurrud in th' English language as putt. Belinda called me down ha-ard on it no more thin las' night."

"There ye go!" said Mr. Dooley, angrily. "There ye go! D'ye think this here game iv goluf is a spellin' match? 'Tis like ye,

142

Hinnissy, to be refereein' a twenty-round glove contest be th' rule iv three. I tell ye I used to go out in th' avenin' an' putt me mashie like hell-an'-all, till I was knowed fr'm wan end iv th' county to th' other as th' champeen putter. I putted two men fr'm Roscommon in wan day, an' they had to be took home on a dure.

"In America th' ga-ame is played more ginteel, an' is more like cigareet-smokin', though less onhealthy f'r th' lungs. 'Tis a good game to play in a hammick whin ye're all tired out fr'm social duties or shovellin' coke. Out-iv-dure golf is played be th' followin' rules. If ye bring ye'er wife f'r to see th' game, an' she has her name in th' paper, that counts ye wan. So th' first thing ye do is to find th' raypoorter, an' tell him ye're there. Thin ye ordher a bottle iv brown pop, an' have ye'er second fan ye with a towel. Afther this ye'd dhress, an' here ye've got to be dam particklar or ye'll be stuck f'r th' dhrinks. If ye'er necktie is not on sthraight, that counts ye'er opponent wan. If both ye an' ye'er opponent have ye'er neckties on crooked, th' first man that sees it gets th' stakes. Thin ye ordher a car-redge" —

"Order what?" demanded Mr. McKenna.

"A carredge."

"What for?"

"F'r to take ye 'round th' links. Ye have a little boy followin' ye, carryin' ye'er clubs. Th' man that has th' smallest little boy it counts him two. If th' little boy has th' rickets, it counts th' man in th' carredge three. The little boys is called caddies; but Clarence Heaney that tol' me all this — he belongs to th' Foorth Wa-ard Goluf an' McKinley Club — said what th' little boys calls th' players'd not be fit f'r to repeat.

"Well, whin ye dhrive up to th' tea grounds" —

"Th' what?" demanded Mr. Hennessy.

"Th' tea grounds, that's like th' homeplate in base-ball or ordherin' a piece iv chalk in a game iv spoil five. Its th' be-ginnin' iv ivrything. Whin ye get to th' tea grounds, ye step out, an' have ye're hat irned be th' caddie. Thin ye'er man that ye're goin' aginst comes up, an' he asks ye, 'Do you know Potther Pammer?' Well, if ye don't know Potther Pammer, it's all up with ye; ye lose two points. But ye come right back at him with an' upper cut: 'Do ye live on th' Lake Shore dhrive?' If he doesn't, ye have him in th' nine hole. Ye needn't play with him anny more. But, if ye do play with him, he has to spot three balls. If he's a good man an' shifty on his feet, he'll counter be askin' ye where ye spend th' summer. Now ye can't tell him that ye spent th' summer with wan hook on th' free lunch an' another on th' ticker tape, an' so ye go back three. That needn't discourage ye at all, at all. Here's yer chance to mix up, an' ye ask him if he was iver in Scotland. If he wasn't, it counts ye five. Thin ye tell him that ye had an aunt wanst that heerd th' Jook iv Argyle talk in a phonograph; an,' onless he comes back an' shoots it into ye that he was wanst run over be th' Prince iv Wales, ye have him groggy. I don't know whether th' Jook iv Argyle or th' Prince iv Wales counts f'r most. They're like th' right an' left bower iv thrumps. Th' best players is called scratchmen."

"What's that f'r?" Mr. Hennessy asked.

"It's a Scotch game," said Mr. Dooley, with a wave of his hand. "I wonder how it come out to-day. Here's th' pa-aper. Let me see. McKinley at Canton. Still there. He niver cared to wandher fr'm his own fireside. Collar-button men f'r th' goold standard. Statues iv Heidelback, Ickleheimer an' Company to be erected in Washington. Another Vanderbilt weddin'. That sounds like goluf, but it ain't. Newport society livin' in Mrs. Potther Pammer's cellar. Green-goods men declare f'r honest money. Anson in foorth place some more. Pianny tuners f'r McKinley. Li Hung Chang smells a rat. Abner McKinley supports th' goold standard. Wait a minyit. Here it is: 'Goluf in gay attire.' Let me see. H'm. 'Foozled his aproach,'—nasty thing. 'Topped th' ball.' 'Three up an' two to play.' Ah, here's the scoor. 'Among those prisint were Messrs. an' Mesdames' "—

"Hol' on!" cried Mr. Hennessy, grabbing the paper out of his friend's hands. "That's thim that was there."

"Well," said Mr. Dooley, decisively, "that's th' goluf scoor."

On the French Character

"Th' Fr-rinch," said Mr. Dooley, "ar-re a tumulchuse people."

"Like as not," said Mr. Hennessy, "there's some of our blood in thim. A good manny iv our people wint over wanst. They cudden't all've been kilt at Fontenoy."

"No," said Mr. Dooley, " 'tis another kind iv tumulchuse. Whin an Irishman rages, 'tis with wan idee in his mind. He's goin' for'ard again a single inimy, an' not stone walls or irne chains'll stop him. He may pause f'r a dhrink or to take a shy at a polisman, — f'r a polisman's always in th' way, — but he's as thrue as th' needle in th' camel's eye, as Hogan says, to th' objec' iv his hathred. So he's been f'r four hundherd years, an' so he'll always be while they'se an England on th' map. Whin England purishes, th' Irish'll die iv what Hogan calls ongwee, which is havin' no wan in the weary wurruld ye don't love.

"But with th' Fr-rinch 'tis diff'rent. I say 'tis diffrent with th' Fr-rinch. They're an onaisy an' a thrubbled people. They start out down th' street, loaded up with obscenthe an' cigareets, pavin' blocks an' walkin' sticks an' shtove lids in their hands, cryin', 'A base Cap Dhry-fuss!' th' cap bein' far off in a cage, by dad. So far, so good. 'A base Cap Dhry-fuss!' says I; 'an' the same to all thraitors, an' manny iv thim, whether they ar-re or not.' But along comes a man with a poor hat. 'Where did he get th' hat?' demands th' mob. 'Down with th' bad tile!' they say. 'A base th' lid!' An' they desthroy th' hat, an' th' man undher it

145

succumbs to th' rule iv th' majority an' jines th' mob. On they go till they come to a restaurant. 'Ha,' says they, 'th' resort iv th' infamious Duclose.' 'His char-rges ar-re high,' says wan. 'I found a fish-bone in his soup,' says another. 'He's a thraitor,' says a third. 'A base th' soup kitchen! A base th' caafe!' says they; an' they seize th' unfortunate Duclose, an' bate him an' upset his kettles iv broth. Manetime where's Cap Dhry-fuss? Off in his comfortable cage, swingin' on th' perch an' atin' seed out iv a small bottle stuck in th' wire. Be th' time th' mob has desthroyed what they see on th' way, they've f'rgot th' Cap intirely; an' he's safe f'r another day.

" 'Tis unforch'nit, but 'tis thrue. Th' Fr-rinch ar-re not steady ayether in their politics or their morals. That's where they get done be th' hated British. Th' diff'rence in furrin' policies is the diff'rence between a second-rate safe blower an' a first-class boonco steerer. Th' Fr-rinch buy a ton iv dinnymite, spind five years in dhrillin' a hole through a steel dure, blow open th' safe, lose a leg or an ar-rm, an' get away with th' li'bilities iv th' firm. Th' English dhress up f'r a Methodist preacher, stick a piece iv lead pipe in th' tails iv their coat in case iv emargency, an' get all th' money there is in th' line.

"In th' fr-ront dure comes th' Englishman with a coon king on ayether ar-rm that's jus' loaned him their kingdoms on a prom'ssory note, and discovers th' Fr-rinchman emargin' frim th' roons iv th' safe. 'What ar-re ye doin' here?' says th' Englishman. 'Robbin' th' naygurs,' says th' Fr-rinchman, bein' thruthful as well as polite. 'Wicked man,' says th' Englishman. 'What ar-re ye doin' here?' says the Fr-rinchman. 'Improvin' the morals iv th' inhabitants,' says th' Englishman. 'Is it not so, Rastus?' he says. 'It is,' says wan iv th' kings. 'I'm a poorer but a betther man since ye came,' he says. 'Yes,' says th' Englishman, 'I pro-pose f'r to thruly rayform this onhappy counthry,' he says. 'This benighted haythen on me exthreme left has been injooced to cut out a good dale iv his wife's business,' he says, 'an' go through life torminted be on'y wan spouse,' he says. 'Th' r-rest will go to wurruk f'r me,' he says. 'All crap games bein' particular ongodly'll be undher th' con-throl iv th' gover'mint, which,' he says, 'is me. Policy shops'll be r-run carefully, an' I've appinted Rastus here Writer-in-Waitin' to her Majesty,' he says.

" 'Th' r-rum they dhrink in these par-rts,' he says, 'is fearful,' he says. 'What shall we do to stop th' ac-cursed thraffic? Sell thim gin,' says I. ''Tis shameful they shud go out with nawthin' to hide their nakedness,' he says. 'I'll fetch thim clothes; but,' he says, 'as th' weather's too warrum f'r clothes, I'll not sell thim annything that'll last long,' he says. 'If it wasn't f'r relligion,' he says, 'I don't know what th' 'ell th' wurruld wud come to,' he says. 'Who's relligion?' says th' Fr-rinchman. 'My relligion,' says th' Englishman. 'These pore, benighted savidges,' he says, ' 'll not be left to yer odjious morals an' yer hootchy-kootchy school iv thought,' he says, 'but,' he says, 'undher th' binif'cint r-rule iv a wise an' thrue gover'mint,' he says, ' 'll be thurly prepared f'r hivin,' he says, 'whin their time comes to go,' he says, 'which I thrust will not be long,' he says. 'So I'll thank ye to be off,' he says, 'or I'll take th' thick end iv the slung-shot to ye,' he says.

"'Th' Fr-rinchman is a br-rave man, an' he'd stay an' have it out on th' flure; but some wan calls, 'A base th' Chinnyman!' an' off he goes on another thrack. An', whin he gets to th' Chinnymen, he finds th' English've abased thim already. An' so he dances fr'm wan par-rt th' wurruld to another like a riochous an' happy flea, an' divvle th' bit iv progress he makes, on'y thrubble f'r others an' a merry life f'r himsilf."

"If England wint to war with France," said Mr. Hennessy, suddenly, "I'd be f'r France."

"So ye wud, Hinnissy. So ye wud," said Mr. Dooley. "An' I'm not sayin' that I wudden't f'aget that I'm an Anglo-Saxon long enough to take wan crack at th' Prince iv Wales with a coupli' pin mesilf."

Prairie State Books

1988

Mr. Dooley in Peace and in War
FINLEY PETER DUNNE

Life in Prairie Land
ELIZA W. FARNHAM

Carl Sandburg
HARRY GOLDEN

The Sangamon
EDGAR LEE MASTERS

American Years
HAROLD SINCLAIR

The Jungle
UPTON SINCLAIR